SANITY Savers

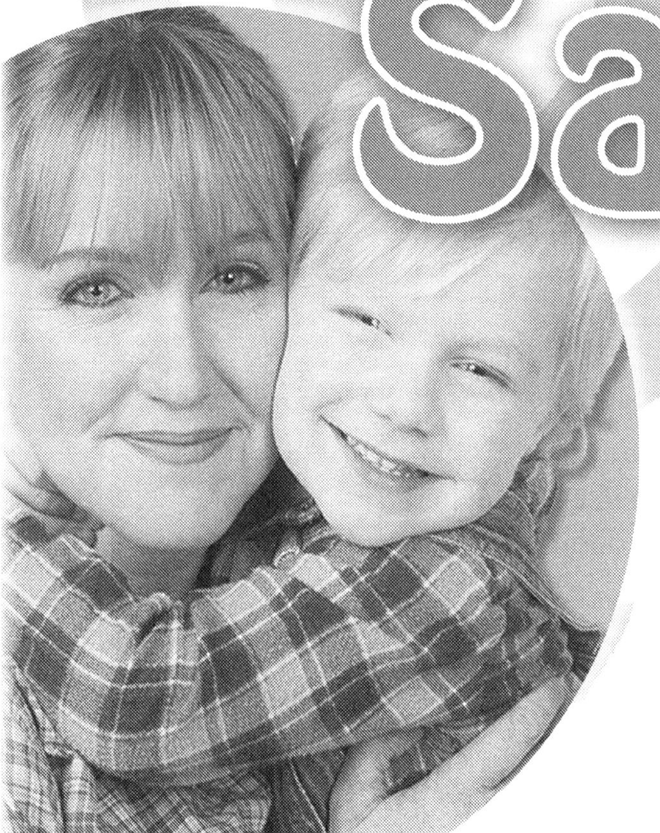

Susan L. Lingo

Susan Lingo Books™

www.susanlingobooks.com

> For we are God's workmanship, created in Christ Jesus to do good works, which God prepared in advance for us to do.
> —Ephesians 2:10

Sanity Savers
© 2007 Susan L. Lingo

Published by Susan Lingo Books, Loveland, Colorado 80538.
All rights reserved. No part of this book may be reproduced in any manner without written permission from the publisher, except where noted in the text and in the case of brief quotations embodied in critical articles and reviews.

Interior design and cover by Susan L. Lingo

All Scripture quotations, unless otherwise noted, are taken from the HOLY BIBLE, NEW INTERNATIONAL VERSION®, NIV®. Copyright © 1973, 1978, 1984 by International Bible Society. Used by permission of Zondervan Publishing House. All rights reserved.

16 15 14 13 12 11 10 09 08 07   5 4 3 2 1
ISBN 980-0-9760696-2-1
Printed in the United States of America

Contents

Introduction 7

Section 1: The Creative Crafts Box 9

Swat That Fly! 14
Apple of My Eye 15
Batik Mystique 16
Spoon Tunes 17
Merry Mr. Zock 18
Follow-Me Flutters 19
Angels, Angels Everywhere! 20
Chalking It Up 21
Finger Paint Prints 22
Ali Alligator 23
Crazy Caps 'n Howdy Hats 24
String Things 25
Stuffy Fish 26
Shivery Snowballs 28
Lots, Lots o' Dots! 29
Gingerbread Drizzlers 30
Rainbows 'n Rain 32
Marvelous Mosaics 33
Whirly-Twirly 'Pillars 34
Tie-Dye Towels 35

Section 2: The Great Games Box 37

Flying Feathers 42
Pat 'n Pass 43
Squirrel-In-a-Tree 44
Catch-a-Cloud 45
Little Lost Lamb 46
Crazy Hot Potato 48

Boppin' Beanbags 49
Shoe-Be-Doo! 50
Over the Sea 51
Wings In the Wind 52
Over the Rainbow 53
Scoopee 54
Pick-Up Sticks 55
Pebble Paths 56
Tickle Tag 57
Frogs On Lily Pads 58
Bounce-n-Hop 60
Folder Games 61
Noah's Rainbow 62
Ark Animals Match-Up 64
Commandment Match 66
Little Lamb, Come Home! 68

Section 3: The Super Story & Song Box 71

Storytelling Techniques 80
God's Rainbow Promise 81
Color Me, Color You 82
Storytelling Blocks 83
Joshua at Jericho 84
Sensory Story Purse 85
Easter Morning 86
Picture Stories 87
The Lost Sheep 88
Story Scarves: Jonah's Adventure 89
Travel-Time Stories: Millie & the Thunder 90
Story Glove: Little Angel Watching Me 92
Mr. Noah Built an Ark 93
Super Songs & Creative Movement 94
Jesus Is Our Friend 97
Busy Bee 98
The Prayer Song 98

Do You Know Who's On the Ark? 99
Song Posters 100

Section 4: The Special Secrets Box 101

Rainy-Day Bag 104
Agalina Hagalina 106
5 Little Ducks 107
The Old Lady Who Swallowed a Fly 109
Awesome Organization (charts, lists, forms, letters, and other reproducibles) 110
Thumbody Special Necklaces 119
Birthday Box 120
Mr. Hugga Bear 120
Terrific Tickets 121
Line-Em-Up Rope 122
Time-Out Banner 123
Hand Holders 123
Transition Tricks 124
Pompom Pointer 125

INTRODUCTION

SYMPTOMS:

Have you ever experienced one or more of the following?

✔ *Sudden bursts of zany energy.*
✔ *Fits of incongruous laughter and mirth.*
✔ *Seemingly tireless zip.*
✔ *Predisposition to caretaking.*

DIAGNOSIS:

A thorough examination of the above symptoms can only yield one of the following diagnoses:

A. You're a bit crazy, or

B. You're a *preschool teacher.*

Let's face it, there are millions of people out there who think you'd have to be crazy to teach preschool. But we're not crazy—we're just *crazy about preschoolers!* And what a delight they are! Bouncy, bubbly, curious, creative, loving, lively PRESCHOOLERS! It does take a certain amount of confidence and loads of patience to go head to head with God's littlest gifts on a daily basis. You have to be smart, savvy, tenacious, tender, and always two steps ahead to survive—and to survive with your sanity! So how do preschool teachers and parents do this? What's the cure? Read on!

THE PRESCRIPTION:

Liberal doses of *Sanity Savers* will help you enjoy teaching, playing with, and working alongside even the liveliest preschool children. *Sanity Savers* centers around a four-part system of resource boxes that offer a complete preschool program at your finger tips. The simple, everyday items for each box are listed along with jam-packed sections containing new ideas, fresh activities, clever games, creative crafts, super storytelling techniques, and invaluable hints, helps, and tips. More than enough material to last for years, and mobile enough to change classrooms in a snap!

Go a little wild with the activities. Get a little zany with your kids. And have a great time teaching preschool while saving your sanity!

What's more fun than creating something colorful and bright?

The words, "I made it myself!" from a proud preschooler! Arts and crafts play a vital role in any preschool classroom, yet many teachers cringe at the thought of doing much more than coloring pages or macaroni paper plates. Excuses for these "artful dodgers" include: "Far too messy, too much trouble, and classroom cleanup is often double!" Yet with truly age-appropriate craft ideas and just the right tips and tools, your time, trouble, and mess are far less! In this chapter you'll discover fresh, exciting, no-mess, less-mess ideas for arts and crafts projects, instant clean-ups, and stress-free preparation. So instead of small messes, you'll be making big smiles!

What are the differences between arts and crafts?

Most people use the terms "arts" and "crafts" interchangeably, but there are distinct differences. Art is defined more by the imagination, while crafts by aptitude and dexterity. Art is the free-flow of expression, concept, and creation. In opposition, crafts rely on patterns for expression. A good example of preschool art can be seen in handing a child cotton balls, paper, glue, and feathers and encouraging free expression through color, pattern, size, and design. What do you have when you're through? A duck, a snowman, or maybe even a crazy car. The possibilities are limited only by the child's imagination! An example of a craft using the same materials might be cotton ball chicks with black paper eyes and orange beaks modeled from a teacher-made sample. What do you have when you're through? An entire flock of cookie-cutter chicks, each with the same paper eyes and beaks.

So which is best: Arts or crafts? Both! Just as there are a variety of learning modes to accommodate children's learning styles, arts and crafts play equally important roles in children's development as well. You can think of it as this: art is born from emotion and expressed through hands. Crafts are born in the hands and expressed through emotions. Some children are naturally creative and express themselves through imagination and emotion. Others crave the security of creating a "something" that has a definite shape and appearance. This is why it's important to offer a wide variety of arts and crafts projects to your preschoolers. The key isn't the project, but the choice! Set out materials and a sample of the cotton ball chick, then give preschoolers the option to make chicks like the model or create something unique. The goal of both arts and crafts is pride of expression and satisfaction of creation. Remember, even God saw that His creation was good!

How are arts and crafts related to preschoolers' development?

Out of a child's basic physical, emotional, and mental sensations come an awareness of self. Just as all young children go through stages in self development, preschoolers travel through stages in their ability to create. The following are brief descriptions of these stages and ages they're most likely to occur.

STAGE 1: SCRIBBLINGS. Two-year-olds make free scibblings which fall into twenty basic shapes consisting of repetitive outlines. Look at the variety of scribbles most often made:

These scribblings aren't symbolic of particular objects or shapes, but are more a means of manipulating mediums such as pencils, crayons, or markers. Because a two-year-old has limited fine motor skills, repetition of shape and line are inevitable—and keep budding "creativity" at a lower level. Expect young preschoolers to find joy in manipulating color and texture rather than creating defined shapes in their pictures.

STAGE 2: DIAGRAMS. Scribblings eventually begin to take the shape of more defined shapes such as circles, squares, and simple X's. Three-year-olds typically incorporate many of these simple line diagrams into their pictures and paintings. Since there are fewer lines involved and drawings become more symmetrical, young children begin to associate names of shapes with their diagrams. Ask a two-year-old to draw a square and chances are you'll end up with a repetitive scribble. But a three-year-old can draw a simple square because he or she is able to remember the defined shape.

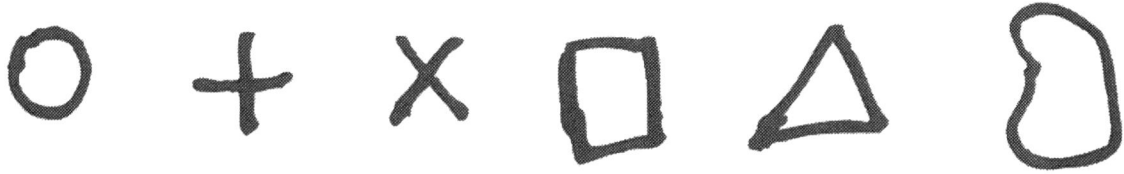

STAGE 3: COMPLEX DIAGRAMS. By the time a child reaches his or her fourth birthday, many changes have occurred in creativity and it's expression. Late three- and early four-year-olds learn to combine two or three diagrams into complex shapes and interesting patterns. And something equally delightful is happening: the preschooler suddenly begins explaining his or her artwork! An expanding vocabulary gives way to verbal and well as creative expression. Suddenly it's not just a simple scribble—it's a castle where a beautiful princess and her white pony live! Complex diagrams are the beginning stage of true artistic and creative expression.

STAGE 4: REPRESENTATIONAL AGGREGATES. The next stage in preschool art is the representational aggregate where three or more diagrams are combined to make elaborate patterns. These patterns represent people and objects born in a child's experience or imagination. Four- and five-year-old art falls into this stage which is the precursor to free creation and symbolism in arts and crafts

The most beautiful thing about preschool arts and crafts is their expression of a genuine naivete of perception in which the preschooler sees the world in a fresh, new way. The key in offering rich opportunities to explore preschoolers' creativity is through quality arts and crafts projects which are as fun to do as they are simple to prepare. Read on to discover how you can pull an entire "art class" together in a box!

WHAT'S IN THE CREATIVE CRAFTS BOX?

The *Creative Crafts Box* is a treasure-trove of arts and crafts items that allow you to offer your preschoolers creative projects in a snap. Every art and craft idea included in this chapter uses one or more of the items found in the *Creative Crafts Box*. Simply choose the project, set out the items you need, and watch children beam! When an item is used up, replace it immediately so you're always prepared.

On the next page is a list of items you'll need to collect. Standard classroom supplies are not included as you will probably have these items in your room anyway. (Standard items include: scissors, white drawing paper, crayons and markers, glue, glue sticks, newspapers, pencils, clear tape, and other like staples. You can also keep extras in your crafts box.)

Collect the items, decorate a colorful box, and you'll be ready for loads of crafty learning times—and pleased smiles!

- colored and white chalk
- cotton balls
- cotton swabs
- empty spools of thread
- food coloring
- glue (white craft glue in several small bottles; tacky craft glue; glue sticks)
- liquid starch
- paintbrushes
- muffin pans (2)
- glitter glue
- hole punch
- manila paper, newsprint
- construction paper
- white and colored tissue paper
- paper towels
- wet wipes
- aluminum foil
- clothespins (hinge-style)
- sponges (several)

- plastic drinking straws
- plastic tray
- foam meat trays (3-5)
- powdered tempera paints
- water color paints
- string, yarn, fishing line
- paper plates, cups, bowls
- plastic spoons and knives
- craft sticks
- chennile wires
- ribbon, lace, rickrack
- plastic fly swatters
- spray bottles
- crepe paper
- paper sacks
- modeling dough, clay
- waxed paper

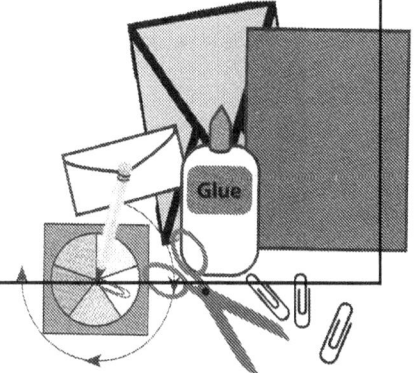

Swat That Fly!

Little ones go "buggy" over this crazy, outdoor painting project!

From the Creative Crafts Box

You'll need several plastic fly-swatters, tempera paints, black markers, white paper, and Styrofoam meat trays.

Setting It Up

Cover the bottoms of the foam meat trays with tempera paints. Use a variety of colors. Place the plastic fly-swatters by the paint trays. Be sure children are wearing paint shirts.

Sharing the Fun

Hand each child a sheet of paper and invite them to use markers and crayons to draw bunches of bugs and creepy crawlers. Then have children lay their paper on the grass and take turns lightly dipping the fly-swatters in paint and swatting their "bugs." Be sure to demonstrate how to wipe excess paint off the fly-swatters before swatting! Hang the pictures up to dry as you play a game of Bug Tag. Choose one child to be the Big Bug and tag other "Big Bugs." All Big Bugs can help tag others until everyone's caught.

HELPFUL HINTS!

- Make disposable paint vests in a snap by cutting the bottoms from paper grocery sacks. Cut up the center of each sack, then finish by cutting arm holes in the sides.

- Pick up paint shirts by-the-pound from thrift stores or charitable church members. Wear the shirts backward for the best coverage!

- Add a sprinkling of soap flakes or a few drops of liquid detergent to tempera paint for easier clean-up.

PRESCHOOL POINTERS

Kids love messy projects and doing things they wouldn't normally have chances to do at home. If messier projects make you apprehensive, plan them as outdoor projects and join in the fun instead of worrying about clean-up!

Apple of My Eye

Young children love the whirly-twirly action of these special apples.

From the Creative Crafts Box

You'll need red and green construction paper, scissors, tape, and fishing line or yarn.

Setting It Up

Before class, cut a large apple shape for each child from red construction paper. You'll also need to cut three 3-inch pieces of fishing line and one 10-inch piece of fishing line or yarn for each child.

Sharing the Fun

Set out green construction paper, tape, scissors, and the pieces of fishing line. Hand each child a paper apple. Show children how to cut their apples crosswise to make four slices. Then help children reassemble the slices by taping small pieces of fishing line between them. (See illustration) Invite children to each tear two, green construction paper leaves. Tape the leaves to the tops of the apples. Finally, let children tape long pieces of fishing line or yarn to the tops of their apples, then hang them from the ceiling or in windows.

This craft is especially fun in the fall when children may have the opportunity to visit an apple orchard or farm. Serve fresh apple slices after the project, then repeat the following action rhyme:

Lots of shiny apples hanging in a tree— *(shade your eyes and look upward)*

One little apple says, "Please pick me!" *(hold up one finger, then point to yourself)*

So reach way up on your tippy-tippy-toes *(stand on you tip toes and stretch your arms upward)*

And pick a shiny apple from up where it grows! *(pretend to pick an apple)*

HELPFUL HINTS!
- Use green curling ribbon to add a decorative touch to the tops of the apples.
- Other fruit and vegetable shapes work equally well for this project.

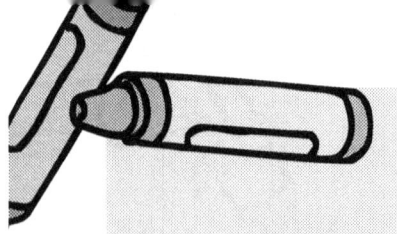

Batik Mystique

This striking art technique was born in India, but will bring smiles of delight wherever your preschoolers are!

HELPFUL HINTS!

- Try using various colors of tempera paint for a really unique effect.
- Light colored crayons work best for this art activity.

From the Creative Crafts Box

You'll need crayons, paint brushes, thin tempera paint, and manila paper or white construction paper. Slightly thin tempera paint by stirring a bit of water in the paint.

Setting It Up

Cover a table with newspapers, then set out tempera paint, paint brushes, and crayons. Be sure children are wearing paint shirts.

Sharing the Fun

Hand each child a sheet of manila paper. Invite children to use crayons to draw designs and scribbles on their papers. When the pictures are finished, have children tightly crumple and smooth out their papers three times. Then show children how to brush thinned tempera paint over their papers. Make sure each paper is completely painted, then set the projects aside to dry.

When the pictures are dry, you'll find a beautiful pattern of "veins" where creases picked up darker paint, and the crayon wax resisted paint. Let your preschoolers choose colored construction paper and tape their special pictures on the paper to create mock frames. Add each child's name to the bottom of his or her frame. Then display the beautiful works of art for everyone to enjoy!

PRESCHOOL POINTERS

Even very young preschoolers appreciate arts and crafts from around the world. Look for simple projects children in other countries enjoy. Be sure to mention that God's gift of creativity is for all people in all parts of the world.

Spoon Tunes

Invite kids to make "musical friends" from plastic spoons—then have a concert!

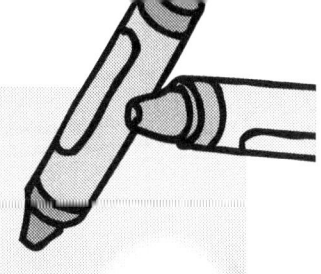

From the Creative Crafts Box

You'll need plastic spoons, markers, tape, and scraps of construction paper, tissue paper, and crepe paper.

Setting It Up

Prepare a sample spoon-tune "friend" according to the instructions outlined below.

Sharing the Fun

Set out the markers, tape, construction paper, tissue paper, and crepe paper. Hand each child a plastic spoon. Hold up the sample spoon-tune friend for children to see, and ask them what kinds of friends they could make from plastic spoons. Allow each child to design his or her own special spoon-tune friend. Demonstrate how to use markers to draw a face on the concave portion of the spoon "head," then use tape and construction paper, tissue paper, or crepe paper to add clothes, hair, hats, or other accessories.

As children work, ask them to make up names for their spoon-tune friends. Encourage children to tell the names of their real friends and why they like those people.

When all the spoon-tune friends are finished, let children have a "musical concert" by tapping their spoons on wooden doors, metal file cabinets, and the floor. Explain that God's love makes us so happy that we want to make special music. For extra fun, play a musical cassette tape softly in the background as children tip n' tap out their spoon-tunes.

Spoons, pots, pans, combs, and other everyday items can turn into great make-a-joyful-noise makers!

PRESCHOOL POINTERS

Preschoolers love making unusual noises and can turn practically anything into whimsical noisemakers! Look for ways to add exciting auditory experiences to your preschoolers' day!

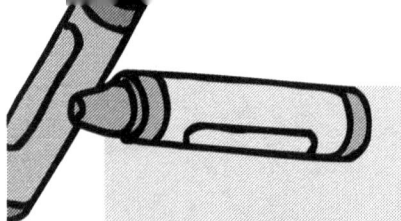

Merry Mr. Zock

Kids will adore this no-fail sculpting fun— and saving their pennies for a rainy day.

> **HELPFUL HINTS!**
> - Squares of aluminum foil make great working surfaces for this project—and a super way to send Mr. Zock home.

From the Creative Crafts Box

You'll need combs, spools, and other "sculpting tools," and self-hardening clay or modeling dough. If you plan to finish this project in class, have each child bring a clean sock.

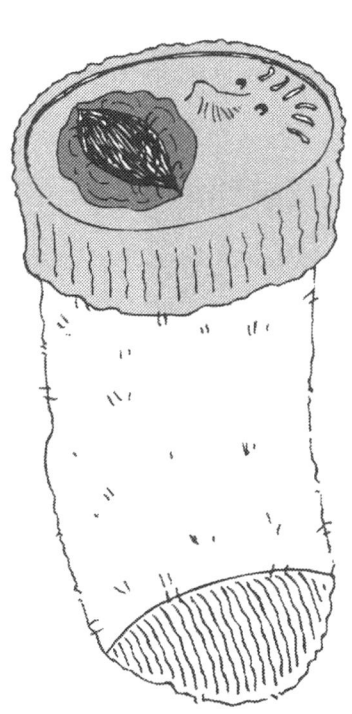

Setting It Up

Prepare modeling dough using one of the recipes at the end of this chapter. You may use self-hardening clay instead of modeling dough. Place a variety of "sculpting tools" such as empty spools of thread, combs, and plastic knives next to the modeling dough.

Sharing the Fun

Hand each child a fist-sized lump of modeling dough or clay. Show children how to roll the dough into a smooth ball, then slightly flatten the ball to make a thick "pancake." Be sure the pancake is at least one half inch thick. Make Mr. Zock's mouth by sticking your thumbs through the lower center of the dough. Pinch the edges of the hole into crazy "lips." Make sure the mouth is wide enough to slide coins through when it's dry. Let children pinch nose shapes in the dough, then use the empty spools, plastic knives, and combs to add eyes, hair, and other facial features.

When everyone's Mr. Zock is finished, let them air-dry or dry in a 200 degree oven until hard and golden-brown. Run a thick bead of tacky craft glue around the inside edge of each Mr. Zock, then attach the ankle of a sock to the glue to make a hanging bag.

When Mr. Zock is complete, use it for a great coin bank to teach preschoolers about saving money.

 **PRESCHOOL POINTERS**

Mr. Zock makes a wonderful, no-fail coin bank for preschoolers to make and give as Christmas presents or Mother's and Father's Day gifts.

Follow-Me Flutters

Preschoolers love this wearable craft— springtime or anytime.

From the Creative Crafts Box

You'll need colored tissue paper, crayons, markers, scissors, tape, and chenille wires.

Setting It Up

Cut two 6-inch squares of colored tissue paper for each child. You'll also need to cut four 4-inch lengths of chenille wire for each child in class.

Sharing the Fun

Set out the squares of tissue paper, tape, markers, crayons, and the pieces of chenille wire. Invite each child to choose two tissue paper squares. Encourage children to decorate their paper squares with markers or crayons. Then show children how to pinch the squares toward the center to create "butterflies." Tape the gathers around the center to hold the tissue paper in the shape of a butterfly. Have each child make two butterflies.

Help children twist a piece of chenille wire around the center of each butterfly to create antennae. Then twist another piece or chenille wire around the center of each butterfly and "wire" the fluttery insects to their shoelaces or shoe straps.

When everyone is wearing a pair of colorful butterflies, encourage children to pretend they're "fluttering and flying" around the room, being carried on the wings of their butterflies. Add lilting instrumental music for a special touch.

> **HELPFUL HINTS!**
> - Black chenille wire adds a realistic touch for the butterflies' antennae.
> - If children aren't wearing shoes that butterflies can be attached to, try "wiring" the winged insects to hairbows, shirt buttons, or belt loops.

> **PRESCHOOL POINTERS**
>
> Any wearable art or craft project is a delight to young children. Something as simple as taping cotton balls to preschoolers' shoes can inspire them to take a "walk in the clouds."

Angels, Angels Everywhere!

Preschoolers feel pride in making these heavenly friends as a reminder that God watches over them.

HELPFUL HINTS!

- Speed-dry your angels by placing them in front of a large fan—but use the low speed setting so the angels don't "take flight!"

- If you want taller angels, simply use tall plastic tumblers and eighteen inch cheesecloth squares.

From the Creative Crafts Box

You'll need cheesecloth, scissors, two aluminum pie pans, aluminum foil, glitter, paper cups, and liquid starch or fabric hardener.

Setting It Up

Cut a twelve inch square of cheesecloth for each child. Cover a table with newspaper. Since this craft project takes some drying time, it's best done over the course of two craft times—but it's worth the wait!

Sharing the Fun

Set out the pans of liquid starch or fabric hardener. Hand each child a square of aluminum foil, a piece of cheesecloth, and a paper cup. Explain to children that they'll be making beautiful angels to remind them of how God watches over us all the time. Have children place their paper cups upside-down on the squares of foil. Then show children how to dip the cheesecloth squares into liquid starch and wring out the excess liquid. Help children drape the wet cheesecloth squares over the paper cups and form them into graceful "angel" shapes with flowing "robes." Let children sprinkle their angels with glittery "angel dust." Let the shapes dry in the sunshine or overnight.

PRESCHOOL POINTERS

Everyone needs to hear positive comments from time to time. Affirm your preschoolers often by making comments such as "You're a real angel" and "Your smile is heavenly." You'll make their day, and it will give you a lift too!

Chalking It Up

This art project gives unusual, textured effects to ordinary paint and colored chalk.

From the Creative Crafts Box

You'll need colored chalk, thick white tempera paint, pie pans, and construction paper.

Setting It Up

Cover a table with newspaper and set out chalk and pans of thick, white tempera paint. Be sure children are wearing paint shirts.

Sharing the Fun

Hand each child a sheet of construction paper. Show children how to dip the end of a piece of chalk into the white paint, then draw with the chalk on paper. Encourage the children to use every color of chalk at least once in their designs. Point out how the paint and chalk combine to make new colors and that the paint adds a bit of texture.

When the paintings are finished, set them aside to dry. After the projects are completely dry, encourage children to trace their designs with their fingers and feel the bumpy paint.

HELPFUL HINTS!

- For an extra tactile effect, add sand or sawdust to the tempera paint.

- Frame the tactile designs to make wonderful examples of "free art" by your peschoolers.

PRESCHOOL POINTERS

Preschoolers love drawing with the soft texture of chalk. Try doodling on sidewalks, scribbling with white chalk on black or blue construction paper, or drawing on wet paper with chalk. All are great effects and provide colorful creations. Spray chalk pictures with hair spray to prevent smearing.

Finger Paint Prints

These colorful prints are a snap to make and offer preschoolers simple, sensory fun.

> **HELPFUL HINTS!**
>
> - Add sawdust to the paint and starch mixture for textured designs.
>
> - Make placemats for snack time by covering dried finger paint prints with clear self-adhesive paper.

From the Creative Crafts Box

You'll need liquid starch, powdered tempera paint, plastic spoons, paper, and a tabletop. You" also want a tub of soapy water nearby and paper towels.

Setting It Up

Do not cover the tabletop with newspapers. You'll be painting directly on the table. If you prefer, use individual serving trays such as you'd find at a cafeteria. Be sure children are wearing paint shirts.

Sharing the Fun

Station each child around the table. Pour about two tablespoons of liquid starch in front of each child. Put a tablespoon of powdered tempera paint on the starch. Have children use their fingers to mix the paint and starch.

When all the starch is colored with paint, let children use their fingers, palms, and hands to make fancy designs on the table. When each child has a design he or she especially likes, gently lay a sheet of white paper over the design and gently rub the back of the paper. Then carefully lift the paper off the table. The design will be transferred from the tabletop onto the paper!

Encourage children to make a new design on the table. Provide additional paint and starch if necessary.

 **PRESCHOOL POINTERS**

While some preschoolers can't be kept out of wet paint, there are some who aren't willing to put their hands in paint for anything! Don't force the issue. Encourage preschoolers to try using just one finger to start with. If this doesn't work, provide painting "tools" such as craft sticks, paint brushes, and cotton swabs. Let children paint designs on the table, then print the designs onto paper.

Ali Alligator

Preschoolers will love this adorable alligator that helps hold their special pictures.

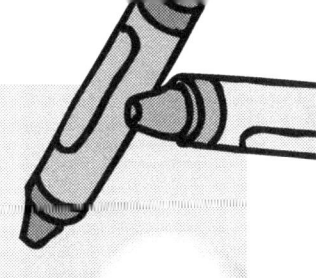

From the Creative Crafts Box

You'll need hinge-style clothes pins, glue, green markers, and brown crayons. You'll also need black constuction paper and a paper punch.

Setting It Up

Prepare a sample Ali Alligator according to the instructions below.

Sharing the Fun

Set out green markers, brown crayons, black constuction paper, and a paper punch. Hand each child a hinge-style clothes pin and invite them to color the clothespins with green markers. As children color the clothespins, explain that they're making cute alligators to hold special notes, message, and pictures. Encourage children to tell what they know about alligators. Remind children that God made all creatures including alligators.

When the clothespins are colored, let children use the paper punch to make small black construction paper eyes. Glue the eyes to either side of the clip portion of the clothespins. Then let children color brown dots and spots on their alligators. Demonstrate how to open Alley's mouth and slide in a piece of paper or picture for him to hold. Encrouage children to take their friendly pets home to hold the pictures they make.

HELPFUL HINTS!

- Use pieces of self-adhesive magnetic strip to make Alley cling to refrigerator doors.

- Make simply wonderful glue dispensers by pouring white craft glue into several plastic baby bottles. Snip a small hole in each rubber nipple, then place the nipple-caps on the bottles. These dispensers are easy for preschoolers to use and you won't worry about glue-pools or puddles!

PRESCHOOL POINTERS

Make your little ones smile by drawing happy faces on index cards and sliding a card in each alligator's mouth as children are leaving.

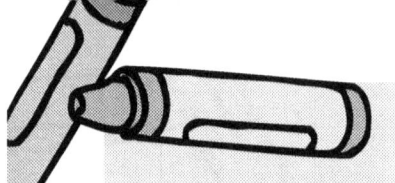

Crazy Caps 'n Howdy Hats

These crazy hats are as fun to make as they are to wear!

> **HELPFUL HINTS!**
> - Paper plates make interesting hats, too. Add a ribbon tie under the chin to keep hats in place.
> - Plastic bowls make jaunty, colorful hats that can outlast even the liveliest preschooler!

From the Creative Crafts Box

You'll need tape, construction paper, paper bowls, and assorted craft items such as feathers, ribbon, lace, crepe paper, and ric-rac.

Setting It Up

Cover a table with newspapers. Set the craft materials on the table.

Sharing the Fun

Hand each child a paper bowl. Explain to children that they'll be making crazy paper hats to wear. Let children tear paper flowers and shapes to tape to their hats. Encourage children to use markers, crayons, and assorted craft items to add finishing touches to their fancy creations. Circulate and make comments such as "My! What a colorful hat you're making" and "You'll look so fine in your fancy hat."

When all the hats are done, have children wear them to play "Hats On, Hats Off." Choose one child to be the Leader. When the Leader says, "Hats on," all children must put on their hats. When the Leader says, "Hats off," all hats must be removed. Switch often until each child has had a turn to be the Leader. For older preschoolers, add marching music to accompany the Leader's commands.

For a festive finale to this activity, lead children in a "Hats Off to You" parade as you march through other classes. Have preschoolers tip their hats and say, "Thanks for being our friends" to the other children.

String Things

These colorful mobiles offer a no-fail promise for preschoolers.

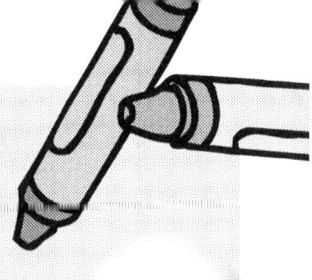

From the Creative Crafts Box

You'll need string, pie pans, white craft glue, powdered tempera paint, aluminum foil, drinking straws, tape, and fishing line.

Setting It Up

Pour white craft glue into pie pans and stir in powdered tempera paints. Use a different color paint for each pan. Cut sting into lengths ranging from six to twelve inches. Cut at least five lengths for each child.

Sharing the Fun

Cover a table with newspaper. Set out string and the pie pans containing colored glue. Hand each child a sheet of aluminum foil and five pieces of string. Show children how to dip their pieces of string in the colored glue, then lay the string in swirls, loops, zig-zags, and other shapes on the aluminum foil. Place the string in a sunny place to dry or use an electric fan to dry the shapes out of reach of preschoolers.

When the string-things are dry, tape each to the end of a piece of fishing line. Then tape the lengths fishing line across a drinking straw. Attach one long piece of fishing line to each drinking straw so it hangs evenly when suspended. Hang the string-thing mobile from the ceiling or in a window. Encourage children to tell what shapes their string-things remind them of.

> **HELPFUL HINTS!**
>
> - Achieve the same interesting effect by using colorful chenille wires instead of gluey string for no-mess, no-fuss fun for very young preschoolers!

PRESCHOOL POINTERS

Offer your preschoolers suspendable crafts often. They love to watch their creations twirl—and it's fun to have a break from typical "refrigerator art."

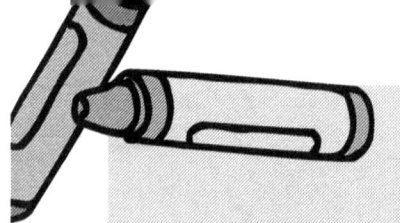

Stuffy Fish
These fanciful, fishy friends will delight any preschooler!

HELPFUL HINTS!

- Write children's names on their fish so they can be sorted out after game time.
- Pin the stuffy fish to a bulletin board to make a great display for summertime.

From the Creative Crafts Box

You'll need plastic sandwich bags, tissue paper, construction paper, scissors, and tape. If you plan to play the accompanying game, you'll need a bed sheet.

Setting It Up

Cut a fifteen inch length of string for each child.

Sharing the Fun

Set out colored tissue paper, construction paper, and tape. Hand each child a plastic sandwich bag. Explain to children that they'll be making stuffy fish to use in a fun game. Show children how to stuff several tissue paper wads into a sandwich bag. Encourage children to use a variety of colors. Close the bags, then tape the opening into a pointed "tail fin." Have children tear small paper eyes and tape them to each side of their fish. Let children add construction paper fins and scales if they desire.

When the fish are finished, play this fun game. Spread a bed sheet on the floor and have children hold the sheet around the edges. Let children take turns tossing their stuffy fish into the "fish net." Make waves with the sheet and recite the following rhyme as you make the waves grow. On the word "wheee," toss the fish in the air and catch them again on the sheet.

Fishy swimming in the sea,

Watch the waves grow higher...wheee!

TRY THIS!

Photocopy the fish patterns on the facing page and cut them out. Let children color the fish, then tape them to one side of the plastic bags.

Shivery Snowballs

This unusual sculpting technique provides preschoolers "shivery" fun—even on the warmest days.

HELPFUL HINTS!

Salt Dough Snowballs

Mix 2-cups flour and 1-cup each of salt and water. Knead in plastic bags until soft and pliable. Form into snowballs. After playing, let snowballs air dry. They can then be "painted" using markers for even more fun!

From the Creative Crafts Box

You'll need foam meat trays, soap flakes, water, a bowl and spoon, craft sticks, and markers. For best results, you may want a hand-held or electric mixer. *(If you cannot find soap flake detergent, make salt dough snowballs. See recipe in the Helpful Hints box.)*

Setting It Up

Mix soap flakes and a bit of water by hand or with an electric mixer until the mixture is the consistency of thick oatmeal.

Sharing the Fun

Place the craft sticks and markers on a table. Hand each child a foam meat tray. Invite children to draw and color outdoor scenes on the insides of the meat trays. Encourage children to include trees, bushes, and houses in their scenes. When the pictures are finished, hand each child a craft stick. Help children put small dollops of soap flakes on the meat trays, then "sculpt" the soap flakes into snow drifts along the ground in their pictures.

Set the meat trays aside. (When the pictures are dry, children can feel and touch the "snow.") As the pictures dry, let children wad sheets of white tissue paper and use their pretend snowballs to act out the following rhyme.

Snowball up (toss snowballs in the air)

Snowball down (let snowballs drop to the floor)

Twirl like a snowflake 'round and 'round! (Turn around in place)

Snowball up (pick up the snowballs)

Snowball down (let snowballs drop to the floor)

Sit beside my snowball on the ground! (Sit on the floor)

Lots, Lots o' Dots!

Preschoolers will giggle with delight over this zany craft.

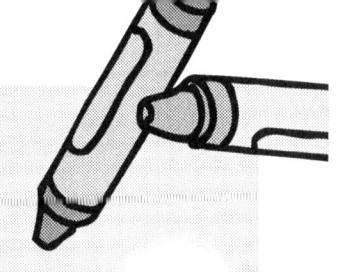

From the Creative Crafts Box

You'll need plastic sandwich bags, construction paper, glue, and paper punches.

Setting It Up

Before class, use the paper punch to make a pile of polka dots. Children will make some of their own dots and spots but your dots will give them a head start-and keep them patient awaiting their turn with the paper punch!

Sharing the Fun

Set out construction paper, the paper punch, glue or tape, and the pile of polka dots you cut out earlier. Hand each child two plastic sandwich bags. Explain to the children that they'll be making polka-dotty gloves to wear. Show children how to use the paper punch to make dots and spots. Then let children glue or tape the dots to the plastic bags. Encourage children to use the pre-cut dots as they wait for a turn with the paper punch. Be sure each child has a turn punching out several dots and spots.

When the gloves are decorated, play a fun "Where's the Dot?" game. Form a circle and choose one child to stand in the center. That child says, "Lots and lots of polka dots on my (fill in the blank)." Then have the child fill in the blank with a word such as "nose," as he or she touches the nose with the dotty glove. All the other children must follow and touch their noses. Then have another child stand in the center of the circle. Play until everyone has told where he or she has "lots and lots of polka dots."

> **HELPFUL HINTS!**
> - Very young preschoolers may have a bit of trouble making small polka dots. Consider using circular stickers for young preschoolers instead of paper punch dots.
> - Children love polka dots! Use them often to decorate pictures, boxes, special bags, or gift wrap.

 **PRESCHOOL POINTERS**

Preschoolers enjoy crafts with a purpose. Use art and craft activities in catchy rhymes or games so projects don't just "sit" on refrigerator doors and fade.

Gingerbread Drizzlers

Preschoolers will be proud to show off these delightful Christmas ornaments.

HELPFUL HINTS!

- Then let children make colorful 3-dimensional designs on paper by letting the colored glue mixtures dribble and drizzle from craft sticks.

- Make lovely gift wrap by drizzling colorful designs on tissue paper!

- Try mixing glue with a variety of powdered tempera paints.

From the Creative Crafts Box

You'll need scissors, white craft glue, powdered white tempera paint, craft sticks, tape, a pie pan, and construction paper. You'll need one sheet of brown construction paper for each child.

Setting It Up

Enlarge the gingerbread pattern on this page and use it to make each child a brown construction paper gingerbread man. You'll also need to mix three tablespoons of powdered white tempera paint in one quarter cup craft glue. Pour the glue and paint mixture in a pie pan.

Sharing the Fun

Cover a table with newspapers and set out the pie pan containing the glue and paint mixture. Place the construction paper, craft sticks, and tape on the table. Hand each child a paper gingerbread man. Invite children to tear eyes, noses, mouths, and buttons from colored construction paper and tape them to their gingerbread men. Then show children how to dip the craft sticks in the glue mixture and drizzle glue on and around the gingerbread men in thin swirls and curlicues. Caution children not to put too many swirls on the gingerbread men's faces!

Set the gingerbread men aside to dry. When dry, tape loops of fishing line at the tops of the gingerbread men to hang on Christmas trees. Encourage children to feel the dried glue. (It will remain white because of the white tempera paint, and look like curlicues of delicious icing!)

You may wish to end this activity by serving snappy gingerbread cookies and allowing children to drizzle *real* icing on their cookies!

PRESCHOOL POINTERS

Read aloud the story of the gingerbread man. After your gingerbread crafts are dry, invite children to act out the story as you read it aloud once more.

Rainbows 'n Rain

Preschoolers adore rainbows as much as learning that God's promises are just for them!

HELPFUL HINTS!

- Cut two sets of colored squares and encourage children to make rainbows on the reverse sides of the paper plates. Hang the colorful mobiles in doorways or from the ceiling as bright reminders that God keeps his promises.

From the Creative Crafts Box

You'll need paper plates, glue, scissors, aluminum foil, construction paper, fishing line, cotton balls, and tape.

Setting It Up

Before class, cut thin strips of aluminum foil. Make sure the strips are at least ten inches long and only about one quarter inch wide. Cut several foil strips for each child. If you prefer, you may use Christmas tree tinsel instead of foil. You'll also need to cut one inch construction paper squares. Cut one square each of the following colors for every child in class: red, orange, yellow, green, blue, and purple.

Sharing the Fun

Set out the cotton balls, tape, glue, fishing line, aluminum foil strips, and paper squares. Distribute the paper plates, then help children glue or tape the plates in half. Let children choose one of every color square and glue or tape the squares along the curved upper edge of the paper plates to make rainbows. (See illustration) Tape strips of aluminum foil or tinsel along the flat bottom edge of each plate to make "rain." Demonstrate how to gently stretch the cotton balls into fluffy "clouds," then glue the clouds to the paper plates between the rainbow and the rain. Finally, cut a twelve inch length of fishing line and tape it to the top of the rainbow to hang from the ceiling.

As children work, make comments such as "God made rainbows to remind us he keeps his promises" and "Rainbows are God's promise not to flood the world again." If there's time, ask children to point out and name the various colors of the rainbow.

PRESCHOOL POINTERS

Model God's faithfulness by keeping promises you make such as reading a favorite story or having a special snack. It's better not to make promises to a child if there's a remote possibility they won't be kept!

Marvelous Mosaics

Even preschoolers with short attention spans go for this art-form.

From the Creative Crafts Box

You'll need colored tissue paper, pie pans, liquid starch, paint brushes, white construction paper, and black markers.

Setting It Up

Pour liquid starch into pie pans. You may wish to cut or tear tissue paper shapes before class.

Sharing the Fun

Cover a table with newspaper. Set out the tissue paper, black markers, and pans of liquid starch. Hand each child a sheet of white construction paper and a paint brush. Show children how to tear small shapes from the colored tissue paper. Then have children dip their paint brushes in the liquid starch and "paint" the tissue paper patches on their sheets of white paper. The starch will "glue" the tissue paper to the construction paper. Encourage children to overlap the patches of tissue paper to create exciting, new colors. Have children cover their entire papers.

When the projects are dry, you may wish to have children use black markers to draw pictures on the mosaics. The black outlines are a striking effect against the beautiful colors of the tissue paper! These make wonderful pictures to frame and present to parents for special gifts.

HELPFUL HINTS!

- Use heart-shaped construction paper and give these beautiful mosaics as Valentine's Day gifts of love.

- For another twist, cut shapes from the dried mosaic paper. Tape varying lengths of fishing line to the shapes, then hang the shapes from drinking straws or clothes hangers.

PRESCHOOL POINTERS

It's important to match preschool attention spans with arts and crafts projects. Too involved a project means an unfinished project!

Whirly-Twirly 'Pillars

What squiggly fun these twirly little creatures are!

From the Creative Crafts Box

You'll need markers, paper plates, tissue paper, glue, scissors, and fishing line.

Setting It Up

Cut a paper plate in spiral fashion for each child. (See illustration)

HELPFUL HINTS!

- Instead of tissue paper wads, try gluing on bits of colored cotton balls for soft, fuzzy caterpillars.

Sharing the Fun

Set out tissue paper or construction paper, glue, and fishing line. Hand each child a spiral cut paper plate. Direct children to draw small faces on the pointed end of the spiral at the center of the paper plate. Then have children wad bits of tissue paper and glue the paper wads around their plates, following the spiral pattern. As children work, circulate and make comments such as "I like the colors you're choosing" and "You're such a careful worker." Explain to the children that they're making colorful caterpillars. Ask children to tell what they know about caterpillars. Point out that caterpillars are usually long and twirly and squiggly when they crawl.

When the children are finished, tape a six inch piece of fishing line on each caterpillar's head so it dangles from the line and twists and twirls. Let the children play with their fuzzy, squiggly caterpillars as you sing the following song to the tune of "Mary Had a Little Lamb."

Ca-ter-pill-ar creep and crawl, (crawl along floor)

You're so cute—you're so small! (wiggle with joy)

Squiggle, wiggle, twist and twirl— (roll across the floor)

Ca-ter-pill-ar fuzzy-curl! (curl into a ball)

Tie-Dye Towels

Preschoolers will enjoy the bright colors in these pretty paper towels.

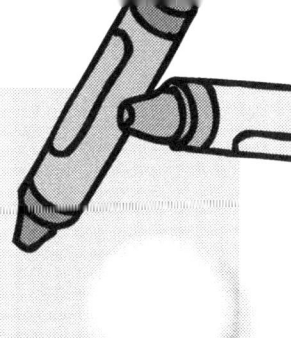

From the Creative Crafts Box

You'll need food color, muffin pans, water, plastic sandwich bags, and paper towels or coffee filters.

Setting It Up

Pour three tablespoons of each color of food coloring into separate muffin cups. Add a bit of water to each cup. Be sure children are wearing paint shirts. Cover a table with newspaper.

Sharing the Fun

Set out the food coloring cups and a stack of paper towels or large coffee filters. Hand each child two plastic sandwich bags and have them slip the bags on their hands like gloves. Then give each child a paper towel or coffee filter. Help children fold the towels corner to corner three times, or the coffee filters in half three times. Show children how to dip the paper edges into the colored water. Then gently unfold the paper towels or filters to see remarkably beautiful designs! Let children make as many designs as they desire, then set the papers aside to dry.

When these tie-dye designs are dry, you may wish to iron them and add frames. These pictures make preschoolers proud when they're on display for everyone to see!

HELPFUL HINTS!

- Do not dip the edges of the paper towels or coffee filters too far into the colored water or they'll turn a brown-black color. Dip gently and sparsely.

- Lay the wet papers on aluminum foil or waxed paper to dry.

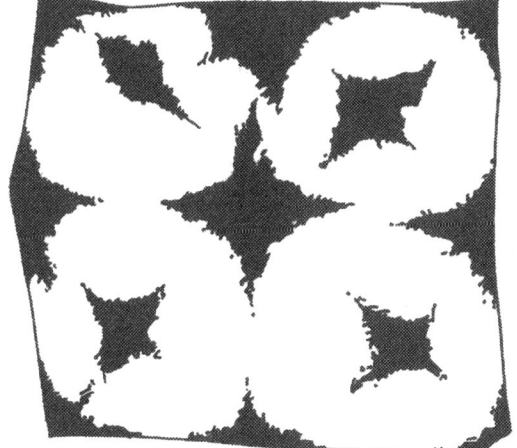

PRESCHOOL POINTERS

Offer crafts that preschoolers can complete and take home the same day—even if you need to send projects on newspapers on in plastic bags to dry!

What time is preschool game time?

When it's time to relax with your preschoolers. When it's time to laugh with, get active with, and get to know your preschoolers. Game time can be learning time and sharing time, discovery time and caring time. In fact, almost any time can be turned into quality game time. You just need the right games at your fingertips—and that's what the Great Games Box offers.

So what do great games offer your children?

A lot! Games needn't be all fun and fluff; in fact, quality games are educational, relational, and entertaining. Young children take games and play very seriously. You can think of child's play as their "work," and preschoolers especially learn three "Skill Keys" from games and play.

1 *KEY 1: MOTOR SKILLS.* Locomotion and increasing motor skills offer preschoolers new opportunities to explore and learn about their world through play. Large and fine motor skills are developing at an astronomic level and both skills are crucial to the whole development of the child. Large, or gross motor skills, include bouncing and catching balls, skipping, walking on masking tape "tightropes," and running in lively games of chase and tag. Fine motor skills include drawing game cards, moving markers on a game board, and drawing scrawly Os on a tic-tac-toe grid. Both large and fine motor skills eventually allow preschoolers to climb to higher levels of play—the predecessors of grown-up pleasure-times which include sports, board games, and the socializing which accompany these activities. Which brings us to the next Skill Key.

2 *KEY 2: SOCIAL SKILLS.* During game time and periods of play, young children learn the give and take of interactive relationships. As much a social activity as any adult party or workplace, games offer young children a chance to understand more about how others react and how they themselves react around peers. Learning "what's mine" and "what I can share" become as vital to social development as numbers are to higher mathematics. And just as learning mathematics comes in stages, so do social game skills. Toddlers and very young preschoolers typically play best by themselves. But by the age of two and a half or three, most preschoolers have moved into "parallel play" where they play alongside others, but not necessarily with them. By three and a half, children are involved in "partner play" and are able to socialize with one or two others in their play groups. And by the time a child reaches his or her fourth birthday, "peer play" takes over and the child is able to function socially in most small groups. Games play an important role in a child's social development and in the formation of his or her personality, which leads into Skill Key number three.

3 *KEY 3: AUTONOMY AND SELF-ESTEEM SKILLS.* Just as a child's social awareness and responsiveness are growing, so is his or her sense of self. It's during the time a child is around the age of three or four that confidence has the opportunity to grow or be squelched—and a great deal of what hangs in the balance is decided through games and play. At this age especially, games that are cooperative and not competitive in nature offer children a chance at "playing without paying;" that is children can play freely without feeling the pressure to perform or the fear of failure. Non-competitive games nurture a child's growing sense of autonomy and self-confidence with healthy fun and learning. Whether it's dropping clothespins in a bottle, tossing bean bags at milk cartons, or running in group relays, preschoolers develop a sense of "I can" rather than "I can't."

These Skill Keys are crucial to a young child's development. The games included in the *Great Games Box* are all designed to encourage growth in each skill area. Read on to discover how to pull your own *Great Games Box* together, then get in the game-groove and move into a great collection of preschool games!

WHAT'S IN THE GREAT GAMES BOX?

The *Great Games Box* is a colossal collection of cooperative games, activities, simple relays, and center games that allow you to offer your preschoolers quality games in an instant. Every game idea included in this chapter uses one or more of the items found in the *Great Games Box*. Simply choose the game, set out the game pieces you need, and have a blast! The following is a list of items you'll need to collect to complete the *Great Games Box*.

• scarves or colorful neckties	• a box of plastic spoons
• foam coasters or disks (6)	• a music box
• cotton balls	• foam or paper cups
• foam packing peanuts	• craft feathers
• beanbags (4 or more) (see directions next page)	• plastic drinking straws
• a playground ball	• several pairs of old shoes
• a small foam ball	• jump ropes (3)
• tennis balls	• a bag of large balloons
• Ping-Pong balls	• several scarves or old neckties
• paintbrushes	• a color cube (see directions next page)
• plastic tumblers (6)	• a number cube (see directions next page)
• paper plates	• an animal cube (See directions next page)
• crepe paper	
• masking tape	

How to Prepare the Color Cube

Gather colored construction paper, glue, self-adhesive paper, scissors, and a square box. Cut six different colors of construction paper to fit the sides of the box and glue in place (one color per side). Cover the sides of the cube with clear, self-adhesive paper for durability. Now you're ready to roll!

How to Prepare Instant Beanbags

Pour dried beans, peas, or rice into four socks. Knot the ankles and trim off excess material.

How to Prepare the Number and Animal Cubes

Cover the sides of two square boxes with white paper. For the number cube, use colored permanent markers to write numerals from one to six on the sides (one number per side). For the animal cube, photocopy the animal patternson the facing page. Color the pictures using markers, then cut them out. Glue one animal to each side of the cube.

All finished? Then don't delay—start to play! Read on for a great selection of games and activities guaranteed to make your preschoolers giggle and grin.

Patterns for the Animal Cube

Flying Feathers

Fly like little birds in this lively color game.

HELPFUL HINTS!

- Colored craft feathers add a great touch and reinforce color names.

- Older preschoolers enjoy the chance to identify colors. Instead of "flying" around the circle, let birds with feathers fly to an object in the room that's the same color as the bird they chose to be.

From the Great Games Box

You'll need craft feathers.

Setting It Up

Clear a playing area in the center of the room. Place the craft feathers in the center of the playing area.

Sharing the Fun

Have children stand in a large circle. Choose one child to be the Mama Bird and stand in the center of the circle. Let each child choose the color of a pretend bird such as red, yellow, blue, or green. (You may wish to use the *color cube* from your games box.)

Tell children they need to remember their colors during the game. Hand Mama Bird a handful of craft feathers. Mama Bird calls out a color and the "birds" of that color "fly" to the center of the circle. Then have Mama Bird toss the feathers high in the air. The birds in the center of the circle try to catch at least one feather before all of the feathers touch the ground. If a bird catches a feather, he or she can fly around the circle one time, cheeping for joy, before placing the feather back in the center of the circle. Then choose another player to be the Mama Bird. Everyone returns to the circle to play again. (Avoid having children choose new colors too often as they'll find it hard to recall which color they are!)

Play until all the children have had a turn to be the Mama Bird and toss the feathers.

PRESCHOOL POINTERS

Young preschoolers often have trouble waiting for their turn—or believing they *will* have a turn. Alleviate impatience or doubt by assuring children before the game that each person will have a turn to be Mama Bird and to toss the feathers.

Pat 'n Pass

Preschoolers learn the concepts of "forward" and "backward" in this fast-paced game.

From the Great Games Box

You'll need one item from the *Great Games Box* for each child in class.

Setting It Up

Place the items from the *Great Games Box* in the center of the room.

Sharing the Fun

Let children each choose an item from the center of the room. Help children form a sitting circle, but be sure they're standing close enough together to reach each other's hands. Explain that you're going to play a game called "Pat n' Pass." When you say "forward," have the children pass their items in the same direction to the people beside them.

Keep passing until you say "backward." Then have children give the items they're holding a pat and reverse the passing direction. Continue passing forward and backward until children are comfortable with the directions. For more fun, let preschoolers take turns being the Caller.

HELPFUL HINTS!

- Until preschoolers "get the hang" of passing simultaneously, have them pass items each time you say "pass."

- If you have a small group, pass one item at a time. When you reverse directions, have the child holding the item say his or her name. This is a fun get-to-know-you game for the beginning of the year.

PRESCHOOL POINTERS

Preschoolers love simple, no-lose games such as Pat n' Pass. When game rules are clear and easy to remember, young children can concentrate on having fun and getting to know each other.

Squirrel-In-a-Tree

This cute game is a favorite with active preschoolers.

HELPFUL HINTS!

- If you don't have enough packing peanuts, use other items from the *Great Games Box*—or use real peanuts in the shell, then snack on them for a nutty treat.

- This is a fun game to play outside in the fall when leaves are crunchy and real squirrels are gathering nuts for winter!

From the Great Games Box

You'll need packing peanuts, paper plates, and masking tape.

Setting It Up

Clear a large playing area in the room. Tape paper plates to the floor around the edges of the room, one plate per child. (Do not tape any paper plates in the center of the floor.) Place a pile of packing peanuts in the center of the floor.

Sharing the Fun

Have children stand around the packing peanuts. Explain to children that these are pretend nuts and they're the make-believe squirrels. Tell children that when you say, "Squirrels, gather the nuts," they're to each pick up a packing peanut, scamper to a paper plate "tree", and set the nut in the tree. Each time you say, "Squirrels, gather the nuts," have children scamper to collect nuts for the trees. Encourage children to find a different tree each time if possible. Play until all the nuts have been gathered and delivered to trees.

Older preschoolers will enjoy more of a challenge. Use one less paper plate than there are children. Each time, one little squirrel will be without a tree. Invite that squirrel to say, "Squirrels, gather the nuts" for the next round.

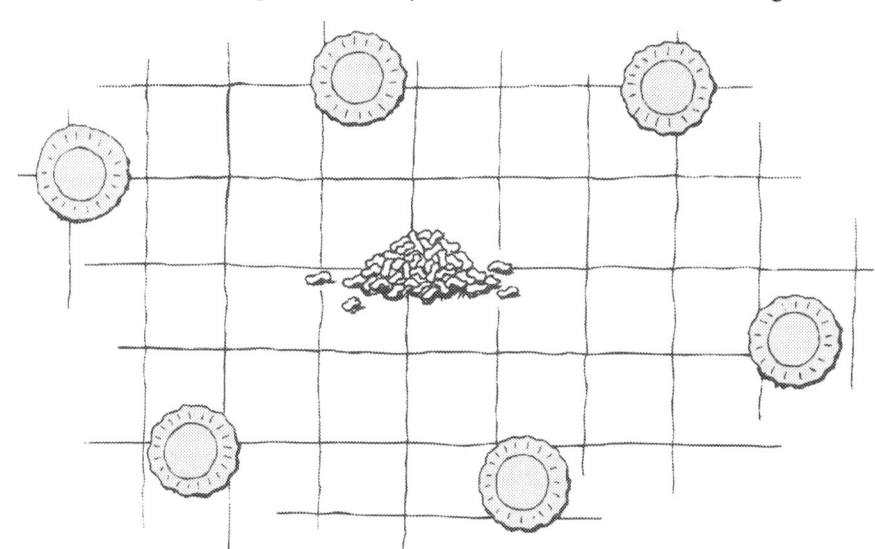

Catch-a-Cloud

Preschoolers love this fun game of imaginary clouds.

From the Great Games Box

You'll need paper cups and cotton balls. You may also want a musical tape or CD and player.

Setting It Up

No prior preparation needed.

Sharing the Fun

Hand each child a cotton ball and a paper cup. Explain that the cotton balls are pretend clouds. Challenge the children to toss one cloud at a time in the air and catch it in their paper cups. "Cloud-catching music" adds a nice touch to this large motor skill activity!

After children have caught clouds for a few minutes, have them get with partners and toss clouds back and forth as they catch them in the paper cups. Encourage children to call out the number of each cotton ball as it's caught…*1,2—fun for me, fun for you!*

HELPFUL HINTS!

- For a twist, have children stand in a circle and start two cotton clouds going in opposite directions. Let children toss the clouds to the players standing beside them in the circle. Continue until the clouds return to their starting places.

- Your preschoolers may enjoy blowing their clouds across the floor in time to lively music.

TRY THIS: Have children stand in a line facing you. Toss a cotton ball to each child to catch in a cup and one to catch in his or her hand. Then move to the next child. Repeat the following rhyme as you play the cloud-catching game:

Catch a cloud,
See if you can—
Catch one in a cup,
Catch one in your hand!

Little Lost Lamb

This auditory hunt-and-find game is a favorite with preschoolers.

From the Great Games Box

You'll need a music box and scarves.

Setting It Up

Clear an area in the center of the room and place the music box in the middle of that area.

Sharing the Fun

Seat children in a large circle around the playing area. Explain that the music box is a little lost lamb and you'll need two "shepherds" to find the lost lamb. Choose two volunteers to be blindfolded with the scarves. Then wind up the music box and place it somewhere in the cleared area. Let the shepherds crawl around the floor until one of them finds the little lost sheep. When the lamb is found, lead everyone in saying, "The lamb was lost, but now is found!"

Choose two other players to become shepherds and repeat the hunt-and-find game. Play until everyone has had a turn to be a shepherd or has found the lost lamb.

For a fun variation, photocopy the lambs on the facing page. Cut them out and hide them in the room. Invite preschoolers to search for the lambs until they're found. You may wish to make a paper lamb for each child to find, then glue cotton balls to the lambs as a quick craft project!

HELPFUL HINTS!

- If children do not like the blindfolds, simply have everyone close their eyes and hunt for the lost sheep simultaneously.

- Older preschoolers may enjoy a special challenge. Instead of hiding the music box, hide another item from the Great Games Box. Then wind up the music box and see if the shepherds can find the lost sheep before the music stops playing.

PRESCHOOL POINTERS

Young c hldren love searching games, but don't hide items in tough-to-find places as this can be frustrating and lessen the fun of the hunt!

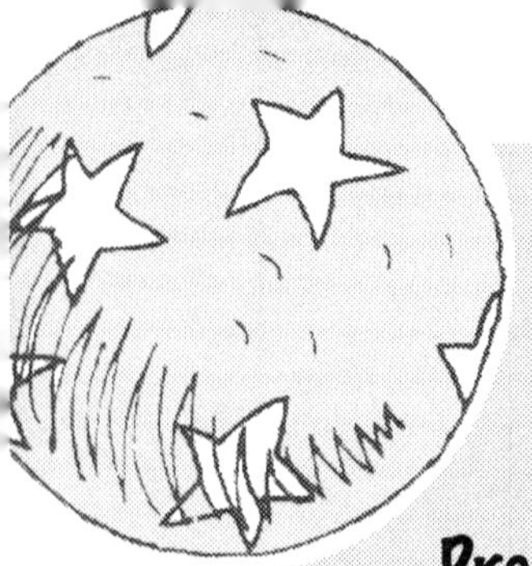

Crazy Hot Potato

Preschoolers will giggle with delight over this twist on an old favorite.

HELPFUL HINTS!

- For variation, make a large making tape square on the floor and have children sit on the square instead of in a circle.
- Remind children not to throw the objects!

From the Great Games Box

You'll need the foam ball, the playground ball, and six plastic tumblers.

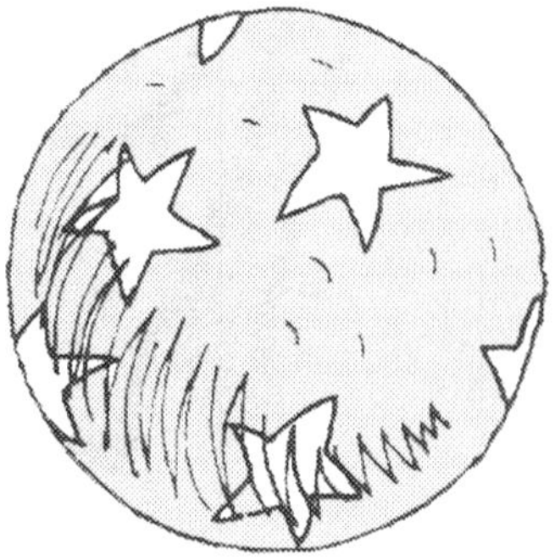

Setting It Up

No prior preparation needed.

Sharing the Fun

Seat children in a circle, positioning them so that their feet touch when their legs are spread out. Hand the foam ball, playground ball, and tumblers to different children. Explain that this game is just like regular Hot Potato only they'll be rolling, sliding, and scooting their objects. Tell children that when a tumbler or ball comes their way, they're to tell the name of a color. Then scoot the object across the circle to someone else. After you've played for a few minutes, have children call out animal names, food items, or their own names.

Try these other simple variations:

❇ Stand in a circle and bounce several balls across the circle to one another.

❇ Sit in a circle and roll balls as you repeat rhymes or sing familiar songs.

❇ Sit in a circle and allow kids ot use only their elbows to roll balls back and forth.

❇ Stand in a circle and count or repeat the alphabet as you bounce the ball across the circle.

PRESCHOOL POINTERS

Young children love surprise elements in games. Tumblers that roll crazily are great fun and never seem to end up where you think they will! For another "crazy roller," try partially filling a beach ball with sand or water and get rolling with some wobbledy fun.

Boppin' Beanbags

Like bowling? Then "bowl over" your preschoolers with this great variation.

From the Great Games Box

You'll need plastic tumblers, masking tape, and beanbags.

Setting It Up

Place a masking tape line across one end of the room. Children will stand behind this line to toss the beanbags (you'll need three). Set pairs of upside-down tumblers about 3-feet from the tape line, and about 4-feet apart. (See the game diagram.)

Sharing the Fun

Form three groups and have each line up behind the masking tape line opposite a set of plastic tumbler "bowling pins." Hand the first players in each line a beanbag. Explain that the object of this game is for each group to knock over their bowling pins by tossing beanbags. Mention that each person will have a turn to toss a beanbag at the pins. When the pins are knocked over, encourage the groups to clap and cheer. Then have the members of each group reset their bowling pins for Round 2.

Older preschoolers will enjoy a special challenge. After bowling a few rounds, turn the tumblers right side up and try to toss beanbags inside the cups!

> **HELPFUL HINTS!**
>
> - If your children are having trouble knocking over the cups, set them closer to the tape line.
>
> - To make this activity more challenging, place the pins a bit farther from the tossing line each time the pins are knocked over.

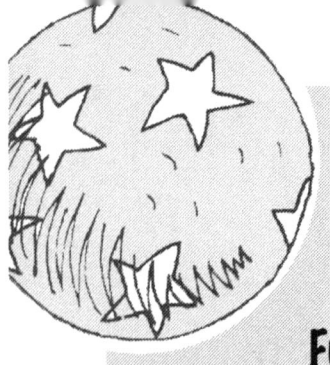

Shoe-Be-Doo!

Funny, old shoes give this simple relay a great twist!

HELPFUL HINTS!

- For a fun variation, let each child slip a shoe on one of his or her hands and crawl instead of hop.
- Check thrift shops for funny old shoes, boots, and slippers (without laces if possible). Store the footwear (except the pairs you keep in your games box) in a decorated tub.

From the Great Games Box

You'll need the Color Cube and several pairs of old shoes. (Refer to page 40 for how to make the Color Cube.)

Setting It Up

Place the shoes at one end of the room. Set the Color Cube at the opposite end of the room.

Sharing the Fun

Gather children at the end of the room opposite the shoes. Help each child choose a color from the Color Cube and tell everyone to remember his or her color during the game.

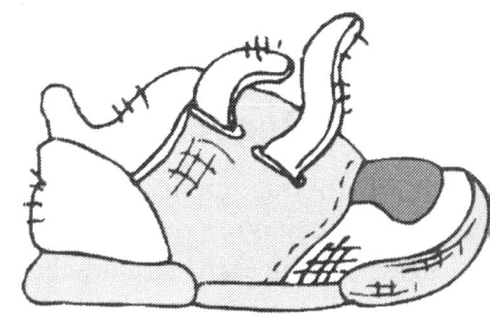

Explain that you'll take turns rolling the Color Cube. The color the cube lands on is the "Shoe-Be-Do color." Children who chose that color can hop to the shoes, put one shoe on, and hop back to the line.

After the next Shoe-Be-Do color is rolled, children with that color can put on a shoe and hop back to the shoe pile. Continue playing until each child has had a turn rolling the color cube.

> ##  PRESCHOOL POINTERS
>
> **Preschoolers adore "dressing up."** Make the most of this fun by using articles of clothing in dress-up relay games. Some suggestions for clothing might include sweaters, mittens, zany socks, gloves, scarves, and colorful men's shirts.

Over the Sea

Play this large-motor game to get the wiggles out.

From the Great Games Box

You'll need a scarf and the playground ball. You'll also need a small table from your classroom. If you don't have a table, children can hold hands to form a bridge.

Setting It Up

Place the scarf at one end of the room, the table in the center, and the playground ball at the other end of the room.

Sharing the Fun

Have children line up behind the scarf. Tell children that they're going on a pretend trip, but to get there, they must go over the sea, under the bridge, and across the mountain.

Explain that the *scarf* is a pretend sea to leap over, the *table* is a bridge to crawl under, and the playground *ball* is a mountain to hop over. Have children travel one at a time over the sea, under the bridge, and across the mountain.

Each time all the children reach the other end of the room, move the ball and scarf a bit closer to the table and travel again. Continue until all three objects are in close succession. If there's time, move the objects farther apart for each trip or add more items to hop over, walk around, or wiggle past!

HELPFUL HINTS!

- Have a simple snack at the end of the "trail." Place a plate of graham crackers at the other side of the "mountain" for children to nibble on as they wait for the rest of the kids to join them.
- Add more items from the *Great Games Box* to make a bigger, more challenging course.

Try these exciting variations!

- **MOVING DAY. Have two children travel over the items to pick up packing peanuts at the opposite end of the room, then travel back. Continue shuffling packing peanuts from one end of the room to the other until all the peanuts are moved.**
- **CIRCUS PONIES. Place items from the Games Box in a large circle on the floor around the room. Pretend you're prancing ponies and trot along, leaping over the items as you travel in a circle. Add music for even more circus fun!**

Wings In the Wind

This musical activity is simple—yet simply fun.

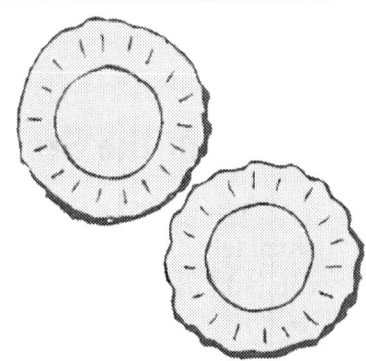

From the Great Games Box

You'll need crepe paper, paper plates, and a music CD and player.

Setting It Up

Tear or cut two 18-inch crepe paper streamers for each child. Have the CD ready to play. Scatter paper plates around the floor (tape them in place if desired or if the floor is especially slippery). For a cheery effect, color the centers of the paper plates.

Sharing the Fun

Hand each child a pair of crepe paper streamers or "wings." Ask each child to think of a flying insect such as a butterfly, dragonfly, or beautiful moth. Explain that the paper plates are fluttery flowers waiting for butterflies and other bugs to come and sip their sweet nectar. Play a bit of "music to fly by" and let children—and their imaginations—fly free! Encourage children to fly to each flower before the music ends.
  Older preschoolers will enjoy acting out butterflies emerging from cocoons, then trying out their new wings. Be sure to play lively music as they "hatch" and fly away!

HELPFUL HINTS!

- After children have winged their way around the room, invite them to land for a special treat. Serve sweet apple juice "nectar" and butterfly-shaped cookies or crackers.

- Keep the crepe paper streamers in the *Great Games Box* to use for other games and activities.

 **PRESCHOOL POINTERS**

Don't overlook creative movement as a game-form for preschoolers! Children love moving to music or pretending to be animals, insects, or fish-in-the-sea. Provide lots of opportunities for children to explore the way their bodies move.

Over the Rainbow

Play this lively game and help kids recognize a rainbow of colors.

From the Great Games Box

You'll need scarves and the Color Cube.

Setting It Up

Place the scarves end-to-end across the playing area. Set the Color Cube at one end of the playing area.

HELPFUL HINTS!

- For a variation, let children pick colors to call out instead of using the color cube. Or roll the cube two times to get two colors moving at once.

- After the game, let children cool down with a cool treat: Rainbow sherbet in paper cups!

Sharing the Fun

Have children stand by the Color Cube at one end of the playing area. Tell children that the scarves are a pretend rainbow. Then explain to the children that this game uses the colors in their clothing. Take a few moments to identify the different colors the children are wearing.

Ask for a volunteer to roll the Color Cube. Whoever is wearing the color rolled can run and leap over the "rainbow" to the other end of the room. As they leap over the rainbow, encourage children to call out the name of the color rolled. Choose a child remaining on the starting side to roll the Color Cube for the next color. Then have children run and leap from both sides. (Caution the children to be careful not to bump into someone else.) You may wish to have to have children hop, trot, walk backwards, or tip toe instead of run.

Play until everyone ends up on the same side of the rainbow again.

PRESCHOOL POINTERS

Games that help children learn their colors, numbers, and alphabet letters are not only fun to play, they're challenging for young minds. Look for ways to reinforce learning through play.

Scoopee

This simple game of skill teaches group cooperation and fun.

From the Great Games Box

You'll need plastic spoons, packing peanuts, and plastic tumblers.

Setting It Up

Place a plastic tumbler for every four children at one end of the room. Place two piles of packing peanuts at the opposite end of the room. You'll need a plastic spoon for each player.

Sharing the Fun

Form groups of four and hand each child a plastic spoon. Tell children that the tumblers at the end of the room need to be filled with peanuts—but can only be filled using spoons as "scoopees." Explain to the children that they'll need to work together to fill their tumblers. When you say, "go," have children each scoop up a few packing peanuts and carefully carry them to the tumblers at the opposite end of the room. Have children pour the peanuts into the cups, then return for more peanuts. Continue until the piles of peanuts are gone. After the game, be sure to praise children for their "team efforts" in filling the cups.

HELPFUL HINTS!

- If packing peanuts create too much static electricity on carpet, try using cotton balls.

- Older preschoolers might like to work in pairs for this relay game. Have one partner be the Carrier and one the Picker-Upper. If a peanut drops, the Picker-Upper replaces the peanut on the Carrier's spoon.

PRESCHOOL POINTERS

Working or playing in pairs is a learned skill—don't expect preschoolers to accomplish pair-shares overnight! Praise, guidance, and encouragement help preschoolers learn how to function in a cooperative group setting and set the stage for more cooperative and interactive play later.

Pick-Up-Sticks

Your preschoolers will love picking up after themselves in this simple, but lively game.

From the Great Games Box

You'll need plastic drinking straws.

Setting It Up

There is no prior set-up required for this game.

Sharing the Fun

Hand each child a small bunch of plastic drinking straws. (Tell children not to put the straws in their mouths.) Explain that this is a game of picking up and counting straws. Count aloud with your kids from one to five or ten. After you've practiced counting, tell children that when you say, "Toss 'em up!" have children toss their straws high into the air. Then clap one, two, or three times (or more according to the counting skills of your group), and have children pick up that number of straws. After everyone has the correct number of straws, gather up any remaining straws and toss 'em again. Older preschoolers will enjoy taking turns being the "clapper" and signaling how many straws everyone is to pick up.

Try one of these variations with your children:

✱ Have children count aloud as they pick up their straws.

✱ Try counting backwards from three or five.

✱ Play with partners. Link elbows and take turns picking up a straw at a time until you've collected the correct number of straws.

> **HELPFUL HINTS!**
>
> - Cotton balls are fun to toss and so are packing peanuts. Vary the game by clapping up to five as children learn their numbers.
>
> - Play a quiet game of Straw-Scraper by letting children see what they can build on the floor out of straws.

PRESCHOOL POINTERS

Games that help children count, listen, and follow directions will help their development skills in so many ways—all the while providing fellowship, friendship, and fun!

Pebble Paths

Leave a trail of happy memories with this quiet game.

From the Great Games Box

You'll need cotton balls and the music box.

Setting It Up

No prior set-up is required for this game.

Sharing the Fun

Hand each child a large handful of cotton balls. Explain that when campers go hiking in the woods they often leave a trail of pebbles and small rocks so they don't get lost. Wind the music box one or two times, then have children silently tiptoe around the room as they drop a trail of cotton ball pebbles.

When the music stops, all the pebbles should be scattered on the floor. Wind the music box couple of more times, then have children tiptoe along the trail picking up the cotton ball pebbles as they go. With the different trails they can make, children will want to play this game over and over!

Try having children play in pairs. One partner will drop the cotton ball pebbles as the partners walk around one area of the room, then have them retrace their steps by having the other partner pick up the pebbles as they return to their starting place.

> **HELPFUL HINTS!**
>
> - Make large geometric shapes from cotton balls such as circles or squares. Then let children step on the cotton balls as they travel around the outline of the shapes. Or use paper plate "lily pads" to let children hop around the room to lively music.

 **PRESCHOOL POINTERS**

Even the simplest of household items make great "toys" and props for games. Cotton balls are super for making "cloud sculptures," silly hats, and hoppity bunny tails.

Tickle Tag

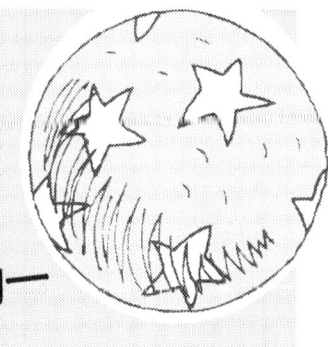

Even preschoolers enjoy a lively game of tag—just right for them!

From the Great Games Box
You'll need craft feathers.

Setting It Up
No prior set-up is required for this game.

Sharing the Fun
Hand one child a bunch of feathers. (Be sure there's a feather in the bunch for each child in class.) This person is the "Tickler." Tell children they can hop or jump to way from the Tickler and his or her feathers. If someone is tickled by a feather, the Tickler hands that person a feather to help tickle others. Play until everyone has a feather.

Try these variations that will tickle everyone!

✻ **Freeze-n-Giggle Tag.** Give everyone a feather. If someone is tickled, that player must freeze in place and giggle for a few seconds. Then he or she can join in tickling others again.

✻ **Flying Feathers Tag.** Give one player two feathers to "fly" around the room with. When that player tickles someone, the tickled player takes the two feathers to continue flying. Play until everyone has had a turn to be the flying-feather tickler.

✻ **Birdie Tag.** Give everone a feather. Tape paper plates to the floor, using one less paper plate than there are children. Call the "birdies" to one side of the room, then call out:

> *Pretty birdies that I see,*
> *Fly away to find a tree!*

Have everyone "fly" to stand on a paper plate "tree." The birdies without a tree repeats the rhyme and everyone again flies to a new tree. Continue until everyone has had a chance to repeat the rhyme.

HELPFUL HINTS!

- Play this game on rainy days when everyone's mood needs a little tickle.

- Consider letting children each have a feather to take home to give someone a tickle—and a happy smile. Be sure to purchase new craft feathers for your *Great Games Box* immediately!

Frogs On Lily Pads

Watch your children turn into happy, hoppity frogs with this active game.

From the Great Games Box

You'll need paper plates and the music box. (Photocopy the frog mask on the next page if you desire. Refer to the Helpful Hints box for assembly.

Setting It Up

No prior set-up required for this game.

Sharing the Fun

Hand each child two paper plate "lily pads". Tell children the floor is a pretend frog pond. Demonstrate how to lay down one paper plate lily pad and hop onto it. Then place a second lily pad close to the first one and hop to it. Pick up the first lily pad and lay it down to hop on, and so on across the room.

Play music on the music box as your little frogs hop around the classroom pond. Encourage children to make froggy sounds. Rrrribbit! Rrrribbit!

Very young preschoolers may need to have the lily pads taped to the floor in a large circle (tape them close together). Let the froggies hop from lily pad to lily pad as the music plays.

HELPFUL HINTS!

- For a tasty ending to your game, serve gummy candy frogs or raisin "bugs." Let children "zap" the bugs from their hands with their tongues.

- Make frog masks by copying the mask on the facing page on stiff paper. Cut out the eye holes. Then invite kids to color the frogs. Tape or staple elastic, yarn, or string to the sides of the masks. Tie them in place so kids can see through the eye holes.

PRESCHOOL POINTERS

Make frog masks and invite children to color the paper plate lily pads green. Then have children take home their very own froggie masks and lily pads to hop on around their living rooms—and to share lively fun with their families!

FROG MASK

Bounce-n-Hop

Preschoolers love counting—and you can count on this game for loads of lively fun!

HELPFUL HINTS!

- If you have a large number of preschoolers, form two groups and use the foam ball in one group. Have this group kneel or sit in the circle.

- Encourage older preschool children to invent their own variations to this counting game. They'll love the challenge of thinking up rules, explaining them to their friends, and then playing their very own games!

From the Great Games Box

You'll need a playground ball (and several balloons if you plan on playing the quieter-bouncing variation).

Setting It Up

No prior set-up is required for this game.

Sharing the Fun

Have children stand in a large circle. Hand the playground ball to one player and ask him or her to bounce the ball several times. As the ball is bounced, lead children in counting each bounce out loud. Then have children in the circle hop that number of times in place or around the circle. Have the player with the ball then bounce it someone else in the circle and play again.

You may vary the game by clapping or hopping on one foot to match the number of bounces. Play until everyone has had the ball.

Play a variation of this game with older preschool children. Have them number off by fives around the circle. Tell children to remember their numbers. Hand the ball to one child and have him or her bounce the ball across the circle to someone else. The person who catches the ball may bounce the ball that number of times to match his or her number. Then have the other children tell what that person's number was. Play until everyone has bounced the ball.

BALLOON BOP-N-HOP. Try playing this same game using balloons instead of playground balls. Have children bop the balloons as other players silently count the number of bops, then take that number of hops.

Folder Games

The next four games are quite different from the ones previously given. Game centers or "folder games" are more "think-about-it" type games and designed for quiet play with one, two, or three children. Game centers encourage calm interaction between children and foster a sense of pride in personal accomplishment when played solo. Game centers are made to use in an instant and are great for rainy days, "catch-your-breath" moments, and for filling those awkward times when mother isn't there yet or sermons are running over.

The following game centers can be prepared as easy as 1-2-3!

1. *Photocopy* the patterns on sturdy card stock.

2. *Color* the patterns and cut them out.

3. **Glue the patterns to file envelopes or file folders.**

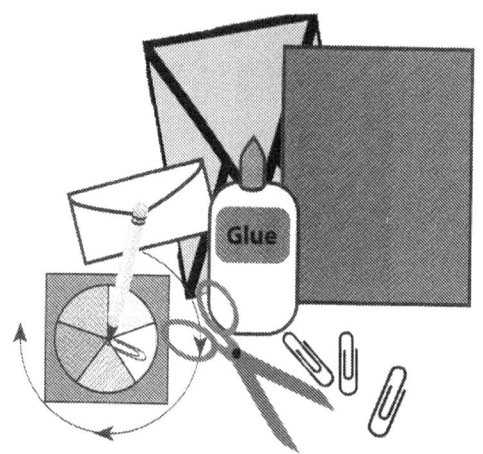

That's it! All directions, patterns, and playing pieces are provided to get you and your preschoolers into game center fun in a snap. You may wish to cover the envelope and any game cards with clear self-adhesive paper for added durability. Be sure to store your game centers in the *Great Games Box* to keep them at your finger tips!

Noah's Rainbow

Learn the colors in the rainbow as you match color cards.

Preparation

1. Photocopy the game board from the facing and the directions box from below onto card stock.

2. Color the game board and color cards.

3. Cut apart the color cards. Cut out the "Directions" box.

4. Glue the game board to the front of a large file folder or envelope. Glue the Directions box to the back of the envelope. Store the color cards in the envelope or folder.

5. You'll also need to cut three sets of 1-inch colored construction paper squares. Use colors to match the color cards (cut three of each color). Store the colored squares in the game envelope.

HELPFUL HINTS!

- Work on helping preschoolers learn to take turns and patiently wait for other players to have their turns.

How to Play Noah's Rainbow

(2-3 players)

Give each player a set of colored construction paper squares. Place the color cards face down. Take turns turning over color cards and placing your color squares on the correct color stripe in the game board rainbow. Play until one player runs out of colored construction paper squares.

red					
orange					
yellow					
green					
blue					
purple					

Red	Orange	Yellow	Green	Blue	Purple

Ark Animals Match-Up
Look for matching pairs—can you find them all?

HELPFUL HINTS!

- Color and glue the animal cards to a paper plate half "ark" as a simple craft project.

- Use a simple basket or box for an ark to put the matching pairs of animals in.

- Let kids use pairs of stickers stuck to index cards to make their own match-ups playing cards!

Preparation

1. Make *two* or *four* photocopies of the animal cards from the facing page and the directions box below onto card stock.

2. Color the animal cards and cut them apart. Store the cards in a large file envelope or folder.

3. Cut out the "Directions" box and glue it to the back of the envelope or file folder.

4. Title the front of the folder or envelope "Ark Animals Match-Ups" in bold letters. (Add animals stickers if desired.)

How to Play Ark Animals Match-Up

(1 or more players)

- Play with a friend: Place the animal cards face down and mix them up. Take turns drawing animals cards and placing them on the envelope "ark." Make animal sounds each time you find matching animal cards.

- Play by yourself: Find matching pairs and place them on the envelope "ark."

- Play with the class: Hand out the cards and take turns finding someone with a matching card. Then act out the animal with your friend.

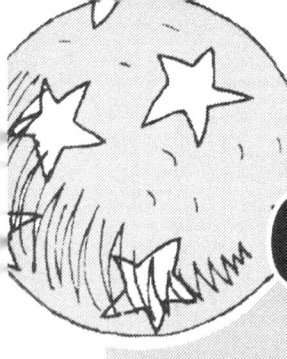

Commandment Match

Match the numbers and God's rules for living.

Preparation

1. Photocopy the game board from the facing page and the directions box below onto card stock.

2. Color the game board and commandment cards, then cut the dotted number cards from the side of the game board.

3. Cut out the directions box and glue it to the back of a large, colored folder or envelope. Glue the game board to the front of the folder or envelope. Store the commandment cards in the folder or envelope.

4. Title the front of the file folder or envelope "Commandment Match-Ups" in bold letters.

HELPFUL HINTS!

- Young preschoolers will need to play this matching game with a reading adult or an older child. Though they may not have needed reading skills yet, even preschool kids can begin to learn God's rules in their correct order.

How to Play Commandment Match-Ups

(1 or more players)

Lay the commandment cards face up. Count the dots on the commandment card and find the matching "stone tablet" on the game board. Place the commandment card beside the corresponding tablet. Ask a grown up to help you read the Ten Commandments.

#	Commandment	Dots
1	I am your God.	•
2	I am your *only* God.	••
3	Don't use my name in bad ways.	•••
4	Rest on the Sabbath and remember me.	•• ••
5	Obey your mother and father.	•• •• •
6	Don't kill anyone.	•• •• ••
7	Be honest to those you love.	•••• •••
8	Don't steal things from others.	•••• ••••
9	Don't lie; instead always tell the truth.	•••• •••• •
10	Don't wish for other people's things.	••••• •••••

Little Lamb, Come Home!

Preschoolers love this simple counting game.

HELPFUL HINTS!

- Simple games with numbered moves help young children learn about following directions, counting, and goals of games.

- Cut out more colored construction paper squares and turn this game into a color game by letting children place matching, colored squares on the spaces they visit.

Preparation

1. Photocopy the game board from the facing page and the directions box below onto card stock.

2. Color the game board and number cards, then cut the number cards from the game board.

3. Cut out the directions box and glue it to the back of a large file folder or envelope. Glue the game board to the front of the folder or envelope. Store the number cards in the file folder or envelope.

4. Place three cotton ball "sheep" and three 1-inch squares of construction paper in the folder pocket or envelope. Be sure the construction paper squares are different colors as these will be used as the game markers.

How to Play Little Lamb, Come Home!

(1-3 players)

Lay the number cards face down. Set a paper game marker for each player on "Start." Give each player a cotton ball "sheep." Take turns drawing number cards and moving your paper square the correct number of spaces on the game board. If you draw the sheep card, hand a cotton ball sheep to another player. If you have don't have a sheep, you may take a cotton ball sheep from someone else. Play until you reach "Home."

The Super Story & Song Box

Are stories and songs that important?

You better believe it! Jesus himself knew the value of effective storytelling to get across powerful points. Jesus recognized that before application can occur, there has to be comprehension. And before comprehension, a specific point must be taught through some memorable means. The result? Jesus' parables! Think for a moment of Christ's parables and object lessons. Visualize the shepherd searching for his lost sheep; the tiny mustard seed reaching maturity in a mighty tree; the Good Samaritan bending over the injured man. Got the picture? Now what lesson or point was being taught in each? You can probably retell the stories and their lessons without much trouble or extensive Bible consultation. Why? Because you related to them! Effective stories and songs paint visual images and stimulate emotional responses through use of common objects and shared experiences. And when preschoolers are especially visual and highly emotional, what better means than through stories and songs for little ones to learn important lessons?

How do I offer memorable stories and songs to preschoolers?

There are jillions of ways to present stories and songs, and a sampling of them will be shared in the following pages. But regardless of the means, all preschool stories and songs must meet the four "V's" of storytelling:

Vocabulary. Present stories that use simple words and easily understood concepts. A typical three year old only has a vocabulary of about 1000 words, so keep story and song texts simple and uncluttered.

Visual effects. Ever notice how most books for young children contain numerous, colorful illustrations? For good reason! Young children are visual learners and because of limited experiences, need concrete pictures they can relate to. Make sure all stories and most song lyrics have accompanying illustrations. Preschoolers love 'em-and recall 'em!

InVolvement. Okay, so the word "involvement" doesn't begin with the letter "V." But the word does begin with "I" and that's what *involvement* is all about. Preschoolers need to be actively involved and engaged in stories and songs before effective learning takes place. For example, giving cue words in a story with accompanying actions makes the story more experiential and loads of fun to tell and hear.

Variety. Have you ever heard a friend tell the same story over and over using nearly the same words each time? It can very boring—and frustrating! Preschoolers become no less bored with the same story and story medium over and over. That's not to say that repetition isn't good; in fact, it's great—and young children thrive on it. But there's a difference between retelling a story until it's stale and keeping it fresh and alive in new ways. For example, you can spice up the Christmas story by telling it with pictures. Or acting it out. Or creating colorful puppets to tell the story. Or using sensory items to enhance the words. Or any number of unique variations. With variation, stories and songs come alive, become immeasurably memorable, and great fun to tell!

> **Kids of all ages, including preschoolers, enjoy the way rhyming words and alliteration roll off their tongues and will pick up on story, song, and poem texts quickly when rhyme is implemented.**

Ready for some engaging storytelling and song times? Keep reading to get the whole *story* on pulling an entire story and song amphitheater together in a box!

THE SUPER STORY & SONG BOX

The Super Story & Song Box is a great collection of storytelling props and pictures that allow you to offer preschoolers memorable stories and songs in a snap. Every storytelling and song idea included in this chapter uses one or more of the items or picture patterns found in the Super Story & Song Box. Simply choose a story or song, set out the props you need, and engage your preschoolers in learning fun. The following is a list of items you'll need to collect or prepare. Directions for the sound-effects recording and the Story Folder are found on the following page.

- several scarves
- crepe paper
- construction paper
- several pairs of gloves
- felt craft squares (1 per child)
- a large purse or festive sack
- masking tape
- craft sticks
- plastic spoons
- markers
- sticky tack (reuseable adhesive)
- paper plates

- plastic farm animals
- a plastic boat
- plastic figurines of people
- an apron with large pockets
- a bolt of ribbon
- scissors
- wooden building blocks
- a musical CD or tape
- a CD or tape player
- a sound-effects recording (see directions on the next page)
- Story Folder (see directions on the next page)

Sound Effects Recording. This is an invaluable resource and is usable throughout your entire curriculum in imaginative ways! Visit your local library and request recordings of various sound effects including: tool sounds, animal sounds, storm sound, traffic sounds, laughter, babies crying, musical instruments, and crowd sounds. Simply re-record the sound effects onto a cassette tape. Or record sounds from your computer onto a CD. Check your stores for sound-effects recordings that are already made. (Be sure to list the sounds in the order they're recorded for easy retrieval.) Store the recording in your Super Story & Song Box along with a CD or tape player to enhance and enrich stories and role-play.

Story Folder. The Story Folder patterns found on pages 75-79 are usable with nearly any story and storytelling techniques included in this book and others. Decide what sizes to make your patterns, then photocopy them on stiff paper (such as card stock). Color color the patterns using markers or crayons and cut them out. (Covering the story figures with clear, self-adhesive paper makes them more durable and fade resistant.) Check out coloring books and activity books for additional patterns that can be cut out and then glued to card stock or poster board. You may want to make duplicate photocopies of your patterns as some stories may call for multiple characters.

To attach patterns to aprons, craft sticks, wooden blocks, or other mediums, simply use sticky-tack or small pieces of self-adhesive hook-and-loop fastener. Sticky-tack is available at most craft stores, office supply stores, and general merchandise centers. Store the prepared patterns in your Story Folder for quick retrieval to use often with stories, games, songs, rhymes, and more!

Permission to photocopy for church, school, or home use only. Taken from *Sanity Savers*
© Susan Lingo, Susan Lingo Books, 2007.

Permission to photocopy for church, school, or home use only. Taken from *Sanity Savers* © Susan Lingo, Susan Lingo Books, 2007.

Permission to photocopy for church, school, or home use only. Taken from *Sanity Savers*
© Susan Lingo, Susan Lingo Books, 2007.

Permission to photocopy for church, school, or home use only. Taken from *Sanity Savers*
© Susan Lingo, Susan Lingo Books, 2007.

STORYTELLING TECHNIQUES

Storytelling is as much an art form as it is informative and entertaining. The following techniques, ideas, and storytelling strategies can be easily presented in any classroom setting and provide loads of learning fun for preschoolers with short attention spans. Some of the storytelling techniques in the following pages come complete with sample stories, poems, or action rhymes to get you started. Use your ingenuity and creativity to implement the strategies in a wide variety of ways and with countless stories and rhymes. You're only limited by your own imagination!

WEARABLE STORY EASELS

What's more fun than hearing a story? Wearing a story! Wearable story easels are novel, and allow preschoolers to take an active role in storytelling. To make these unique easels, purchase a twelve inch felt craft square for each child in class and one for yourself. Felt craft squares are found in any craft store and are quite inexpensive. Black, dark blue, or gray felt squares work best. Attach the felt squares to children's tummies by taping them to shirts or using safety pins. Choose the story patterns you'll need from the Story Folder or create your own characters and shapes from stiff paper. Glue a bit of felt on the back of each pattern piece. Then tell the story as you hand different children the pictures. Have children "stick" the pictures to the felt squares. When the story is finished, invite children to tell what story piece they have and answer questions about that character.

Wearable story easels are also great tools for reviewing stories, lessons learned, and playing games. For example, help children stand in sequence of the story pictures, then encourage children to retell the story in their own words! Or play "story land safari" and hide story pictures around the room. Then invite children to find the pictures and "capture" them by sticking the pictures to their felt squares.

Wearable story easels are great fun to use as children sit in a circle. Children can easily see every picture simultaneously, and little hands and growing minds are kept actively involved. Songs and stories that involve shapes and colors lend themselves especially well to this fun medium. For example, cut out sets of colorful circle dots for each child. As color words are said or sung, let children attach the correct colors to their tummies.

The following are examples of a story and song to use with wearable story easels.

God's Rainbow Promise

Read the story below. When you come to an underlined word, place the corresponding pattern or item on the felt.

<u>God</u> told <u>Noah</u>, "My <u>heart's</u> with pain.

People are bad, so I'll make it rain.

I'll flood the world and wash it, you see,

But you'll be safe because you love me!"

Then God told Noah to build a <u>boat</u>

To carry the animals so they'd float.

In came the <u>ram</u>, and in came the <u>sheep</u>.

In came the <u>cow</u> and <u>dove</u>—tweet, tweet!

Every animal came on inside (make animal sounds)

And stayed safe and dry on their watery ride. (Rock back and forth)

It rained and it poured for many a day,

But God kept them safe and hidden away. (Cover your eyes)

Then the rain finally stopped and, my oh my!

God put a <u>rainbow</u> up high in the sky!

With <u>yellow</u> and <u>red</u> and <u>green</u> and <u>blue</u> (hold up the colored dots)

And <u>purple</u> and <u>orange</u>—God made it for you!

The world was clean when God stopped the rain,

And he promised to never flood it again! (Cover your hearts with your hands)

Story Folder

Patterns you'll need from the Story Folder:
- "God" star burst
- boat
- man
- cow
- sheep
- ram
- dove
- sun
- heart
- rainbow

You'll also need color dots for each child (red, yellow, green, blue, purple, orange).

Color Me, Color You

Songs

Sing the following song to the tune of "Mary Had a Little Lamb." When you come to an underlined word, place the corresponding color on the felt.

Story Folder

You'll need shapes or dots in the following colors:

- red
- yellow
- green
- blue
- purple
- orange

Use paint brush shapes or a rainbow for even more fun!

Color me and color you,
Color <u>red</u> and color <u>blue</u>.
I love God and I love you, (point upward, then to a friend)
Color, color me.

Color you and color me,
Color <u>yellow</u>, color <u>green</u>.
I love God and he loves me, (point upward, then to yourself)
Color, color me.

Color you and color me,
Color <u>orange</u> and <u>purple</u>—wheee! (Put your hands in the air)
I love God and God loves me, (point upward, then to yourself)
Color, color me.

Preschoolers love to sing! And learning colors, days of the week, numbers, and even books of the Bible are more fun when they're sung. Let children record their voices and take home the recordings to share the music in their hearts with their families and friends!

Joshua at Jericho

Use the following story about Joshua at Jericho to start you off creating a set of storytelling blocks. Remember, your blocks can be used over and over again with different story pictures. So build some story time excitement and have a tower of fun! Gather children in a circle on the floor. Read the story below. When you come to an underlined word, place the corresponding storytelling block on the floor.

Joshua was God's brave <u>soldier</u>. He prayed and listened carefully to all God's commands—and Joshua obeyed God in all he did. God told Joshua he would give him the city of Jericho, for the people there were mean and didn't love God. But guess what was around the city of Jericho? A big, tall, brick wall! Let's build the wall of Jericho! *(Have children use plain blocks to build the wall.)*

Joshua wondered, "How can we ever get over that wall?" But God told them what to do. God told the <u>priests</u> and <u>soldiers</u> to march around the wall. And God told the priests to blow their horns. Then Joshua led the marching parade! First came Joshua *(point to "Joshua")*, then came the priests with their horns *(point to the priest)*, and last came the soldiers *(point to the soldier)*. They marched around the wall seven times. Let's count to seven. *(Lead children in counting to seven).*

Then Joshua told the priests to blow their horns and bang! the walls came tumbling down! Let's shout, "God helps us!" and knock down the wall. *(Lead children in shouting "God helps us," then gently knock down the plain blocks.)* God's plan worked! Joshua and the soldiers rushed in and captured the city for God. Then Joshua thanked God for his help and love.

Story Folder

Patterns you'll need from the Story Folder (photocopy multiple patterns):

- "God" star burst
- three soldiers
- priest

You'll also need several plain blocks to build a wall.

Super Tip!

Make several copies of story pattern characters so you'll have enough pictures if a story calls for multiples of the same character, such as soldiers, cows, or children.

STORYTELLING BLOCKS

Is there a more imaginative preschool toy than building blocks? Stackable, storable, and incredibly versatile, wooden building blocks can offer the "building blocks" of effective storytelling. Whether they're ready-made or simple lumber-yard scraps, wooden blocks invite a preschooler's touch and stimulate the imagination.

To prepare your set of storytelling blocks, choose ten to twelve large, smooth-sided blocks. Sand them if necessary. Then photocopy the Story Folder patterns to accommodate the size of the blocks. Color the pictures and cut them out.

When you're ready for storytelling, simply use sticky-tack to affix the appropriate story pictures to different sides of the blocks. Place the storytelling blocks in front of the children as you tell the story, much the same way you'd show pictures in a book.

For a fun twist, hand each child a story block and let him or her set out the blocks at appropriate places in the story. Or line up the story blocks in random order and encourage children to pick out the correct picture blocks as you tell the story. Storytelling blocks are super story reinforcers! Challenge children to place them in correct sequential order after a story has been presented. And just letting children play with storytelling blocks encourages them to retell stories in their own words. Storytelling blocks offer variety, child-involvement, and great visual effects for preschoolers—and you!

The story on the next page is a good example of storytelling using picture blocks.

> In spite of their limited vocabulary, most preschoolers love retelling stories in their own words. Storytelling Blocks with illustrations help cue kids in on what happened next which makes retelling stories easier and more fun.

SENSORY STORY PURSE

What preschooler doesn't love rummaging around in Mommy's or Grandma's purse? After all, purses hold such exciting surprises and delightful, hidden treasures. Use this natural sense of preschool curiosity in your storytelling, and you'll be sure to capture children's attention. You can hide practically any story props in this purse or bag but sensory items are especially well-suited for this medium. Any items that can be felt, tasted, smelled, or heard will work. Include items that are natural extensions of the story you've chosen, such as scented tea bags for the wise men's spices, crackers for feeding the 5,000, fuzzy fake fur for Esau's hairy hands, or sandpaper for Jesus' cross.

The Easter story, on the next page, is perfect to use with the Sensory Story Purse!

HELPFUL HINT!

Any large bag or box will work well with this technique. Even backpacks and small suitcases will peak kids' interest!

Easter Morning

Collect the following items and place them in the Sensory Story Purse: sandpaper, vinegar or a dill pickle, a rose thorn, a bit of cloth, crackers, a paper cup, and a stone large enough to cover the opening of the paper cup.

Jesus was God's Son and many people loved Him. But there were other people who didn't love Jesus. Those people wanted to hurt Him. Jesus and His friends ate one last dinner together. Jesus shared bread and wine with His friends. *(Remove the crackers.)* **We can share crackers with our friends, too.** *(Hand each child a cracker to nibble.)* **Jesus told his friends to remember Him when they ate bread and drank wine.**

Then Jesus went to a garden to talk to God. Jesus loved God and knew He would soon be with His Father in heaven. Mean soldiers came and arrested Jesus. They made fun of Him and made Him wear a crown of thorns. Ouch! *(Remove the rose thorn and let children gently feel the pointed tip.)* **What an awful thing to do! They hung Jesus on a rough, wooden cross.** *(Remove the sandpaper and let children feel the texture.)* **The mean people gave Him sour vinegar to drink. Poor Jesus!** *(Let children smell the vinegar or dill pickle.)* **Jesus died on the cross, and His friends wrapped him in cloth.** *(Allow children to touch the cloth.)* **Jesus' friends put His body in a tomb, and a big stone was rolled in front of the opening.** *(Remove the paper cup and stone. Place the paper cup on its side. Let children take turns placing the stone in front of the "tomb.")*

Jesus' friends were so sad. They loved Jesus and missed Him. Three days went by. Let's count to three. One, two, three! Then guess what happened? Jesus' friends found the stone rolled away from the tomb! An angel had rolled away the stone. *(Have children take turns rolling away the stone from the paper cup.)* **Was Jesus inside the tomb? No! He wasn't inside because Jesus was alive! God raised Jesus from death! What a happy day! Let's clap to show how happy we are that Jesus is alive.** *(Lead children in lively applause.)*

> Let children take turns identifying the items from the story. Encourage older preschoolers to retell the story in their own words using the sensory story props.

AUDIO AND VIDEO STORYTELLING

A discussion of storytelling techniques wouldn't be complete without touching on the area of electronic storytelling. Yes, you do need a plug and electrical outlet, so electronic storytelling isn't as practical or mobile as other means. But for storytelling made quick and easy during those times you're just not prepared no matter how hard you've tried, audio and video stories can come through in a pinch!

Audio stories include books and accompanying tapes, sound effect tapes or records, and recorded stories you prepare yourself. Try choosing several of your favorite Bible storybooks and reading the text as you record them on cassette tape. If you want a real challenge, insert noises you generate or record from a sound effects record. Be sure to include page-turn clangs to clue readers into appropriate times to turn the pages of the story. Before you know it, you'll be an audio recording engineer! Keep your recorded stories handy and play the text as you show children the pictures. It's a fun twist to favorite stories and helps when you have laryngitis or want to offer preschoolers fine listening centers. To create a listening center, simply set out a cassette player and a storybook, then begin the recording. Kids will know when to turn the pages by your recorded signals.

Video storytelling is a bit more limiting as most of us can't generate our own video cassette tapes or CD-ROM's. Check garage sales, bookstores, and discount houses for videos. You'll be surprised how inexpensively they can be purchased. Consider inviting your preschoolers to bring a list of the videos they have at home and would be willing to share with the class upon occasion. Know I know many teachers and parent balk at the idea of setting preschoolers in front of a the television for a video. "Not enough human contact" so it goes. I agree if that's all you're planning for story time. But the occasional use of a video is actually a plus for most preschoolers. Remember the fourth "V" in the four "V's" of Storytelling? Variety! And videos, when used with other storytelling mediums, add exciting variety and animation other mediums can't offer. So don't be afraid to "turn 'em on" to story time with exciting electronic storytelling as one option.

PICTURE STORIES

What are picture stories? Just what you'd think—stories that use pictures instead of certain words. Since young children are concrete thinkers, using pictures to represent certain words helps them "tell" the story without having advanced reading skills.

Get the "picture?" Rebus stories are involving, fun-to-hear, and encourage young children to help "read" along with the storyteller. And oh, the smiles you'll see from proud preschoolers who enjoy this special kind of "reading!" All stories can be presented in the Rebus format. That's right—all stories! Choose a story to read or tell, then sketch or cut out ready-made pictures that are able to substitute for some of the words. Nature objects, animals, houses, people, cars and boats, and number words all lend themselves very well to Rebus pictures, and require minimal art talent. Make use of coloring books, magazines, old picture books, old activity books or workbooks, greeting cards, wrapping paper, newspapers, and even fabric patterns for Rebus pictures. They're simple to find, easy to cut out, and so effective in storytelling!

The following story and Scripture verses are here to get you into the swing of using Rebus stories with your preschoolers. Substitute other pictures for the ones given, or enlarge the pictures here to use with the text. Be sure to encourage your preschoolers to tell the name of each picture as you hold it up.

THE LOST SHEEP

A shepherd had **100** 🐑, but **1** wandered off and became lost. The shepherd was so ☹. He wanted to find his lost 🐑, so he left the rest of the flock to look. The shepherd looked ⬆. The shepherd looked ⬇. He used his 👀 to look for the sheep, and his 👂👂 to listen for its baa-aa. The shepherd didn't 🛑 until he found the little lost 🐑. The shepherd was so 🙂! He called his friends to tell them he'd found his lost 🐑. And they all had a party to celebrate their joy!

STORY SCARVES

Story scarves are a unique way to get preschoolers involved in stories and songs. Floaty, flighty scarves invite children to express moods, characters, and other story effects. For example, encourage children to use Story Scarves to express sadness and joy as you tell the Easter story; to make windy waves as you tell the story of Jesus calming the sea; to make trunks, ears, and tails for Noah's ark animals; or to create costume pieces for any other story.

How to collect your supply of scarves? Check second hand stores like the Salvation Army, ask church members to donate old scarves, or purchase several yards of fabric and hem your own. Silk, rayon, or chiffon fabrics float exceptionally well, but cotton and polyester work, too. If you simply can't find enough scarves, long crepe paper streamers make a workable substitute.

Here's a "funciful" story to help you see how Story Scarves work.

Jonah's Adventure

Read aloud the following story. Use Story Scarves to act out the motions.

Once there was a man named Jonah. *(Make a beard.)* **God told Jonah to go to the town of Nineveh and tell them about God. Jonah was scared.** *(Shake the scarves.)* **Jonah didn't want to go. So he jumped on a boat to hide from God.** *(Cover your eyes with the scarves.)* **Could Jonah hide from God? No way! God made a storm on the sea. The waves were sooo big!** *(Make wild "waves.")* **The boat was going to sink. The sailors were angry at Jonah for disobeying God. So they tossed him into the water—kersplash!** *(Wave the scarves on the ground.)* **Jonah sank in the water until it was over his head.** *(Wave the scarves up high.)* **Then, oh my goodness! A big fish came along and swallowed Jonah up!** *(Make big arm circles with the scarves.)* **Jonah was inside the fish.** *(Sit down and place the scarves loosely over your heads.)* **For three days Jonah sat in the fish. He prayed to God. He told God he was sorry for disobeying. Did God hear Jonah's prayer? Yes! The big fish spit Jonah out on a sandy beach.** *(Pop up and wave the scarves.)* **Jonah decided to obey God. He went to Nineveh and told the people about God right away! Yeah, Jonah! Yeah, God! Yeah!** *(Wave the scarves like pompoms.)*

TRAVEL TIME STORIES

This storytelling technique is incredibly simple, requiring only a few moments to prepare. You'll need your Storytelling Folder and patterns appropriate to the story you've chosen to tell.

Tape the story pictures around the room at children's eye level. Then as you tell the story, "visit" each picture location. Your active preschoolers will enjoy the "trip" and stay attentive. For real fun, have them "pack" pretend suitcases before a Travel Time Story. Hand each child a paper bag, then provide a cookie or cracker for each child to pack. Halfway through the story, let children take a snack break and review the first part of the story as they nibble their goodies. Such fun!

Travel time Stories are naturals for fun review activities. Have children stand in the center of the room, then ask a question that has as its answer one of the pictures on the wall. Have children hop, walk backward, or crawl to the various pictures to answer questions. The following story is one your preschoolers will love using with the Travel time technique.

Millie and the Thunder

Patterns you'll need from a coloring book: mouse, pig, and duck. You'll also need cotton balls for clouds and a jagged piece of aluminum foil for lightning. Before reading this story, tape the pictures on a wall in different locations in the class at eye level for the children. Tape the "lightning" by the cotton ball clouds.

(Begin at the picture of Millie, and sit down.) **Millie was a cute little mouse, but she was afraid of almost everything! Millie was afraid big flowers. She was afraid of bugs. And she was afraid of the dark. But most of all, Millie was afraid of lightning and…THUNDER!**

One hot day, Millie went for a walk. *(Walk around the class as you continue.)* **She hopped over pebbles.** *(Hop a few times.)* **She tiptoed in the tall grass.** *(Tiptoe a few steps.)* **Millie had such fun, but she was very thirsty. "Oh, if only there was some water to drink!" said Millie. Then Millie looked up and saw dark clouds in the sky.** *(Lead children to the cotton ball clouds.)* **Suddenly, there was a flash of lightning, then a CRRASH of thunder! "Oh, oh! Thunder!" cried scared little Millie. She started to run.** *(Run to the picture of the pig and sit down.)*

Millie saw a pig rolling in the dirt. "Thunder!" cried Millie. "Thunder!" said the pig. "Thunder, thunder is part of God's plan. It brings the rain to water the land! Now I'll have cool mud to roll in. I'm glad for thunder," said the happy pig. Just then, there came another big BOOM! "Thunder!" cried Millie. She ran and ran. *(Run to the picture of the duck and sit down.)*

Millie saw a duck waddling in the dust. "Thunder!" cried Millie. "Thunder!" said the duck. "Thunder, thunder is part of God's plan. It brings the rain to water the land!

Now my pool will be full of water so I can swim. I'm glad for thunder," said the happy duck.

Millie thought about the pig and the duck. They were happy for thunder. Thunder brings rain—and water. Water for mud. Water for ponds. And water to drink! Millie could finally have a drink of fresh water. Boom! BOOM! CRRRASH! Was Millie afraid? No siree! "Thunder, thunder is part of God's plan. It brings the rain to water the land! Now I can have a good drink of water! I'm glad for thunder," said the happy, little mouse. Millie danced a happy little jig and opened her mouth for a drink. *(Let children hop around with their mouths open pretending to catch raindrops on their tongues.)*

Helpful Hint

Stories that revolve around or have something to do with traveling or moving work especially well for this storytelling technique. The story of Abraham's move to Cannan, the Exodus, and even Jesus' Triumphal Entry into Jerusalem are real winners for Travel time Stories.

STORY GLOVE

Perhaps you've seen puppet gloves like these in toy stores. You can be a proud owner for a significant price—or make your own the easy way! Story gloves are nothing more than stretchy gloves that have pictures which attach to the fingers. Use the pictures from your Story Folder and attach them to the fingers of the glove with sticky-tack or bits of self-adhesive hook-and-loop fasteners. As you tell the story, sing the song, or repeat the rhyme, simply attach figures to the fingers like puppets. I recommend collecting a pair of one-size-fits-all, stretchy gloves or cotton garden gloves. This way you can tell a story with twelve characters. (Remember the palms!)

Preschoolers love watching Story Glove stories; but want to try the gloves themselves with great yearning. Indulge your little ones by supplying each child his or her own "glove." Plastic bag-type gloves are very inexpensive and can be purchased from food suppliers or from most fast-food restaurants. Or keep your eyes open for inexpensive, stretchy children's gloves. (Spring is a great time to find these neat little gloves on clearance!) Photocopy a set of story characters for each child. Then hand each child a set of characters, each with a bit of sticky-tack or tape on the back. As you tell the story, let children attach their own pictures to the gloves. What a great take-home craft—and a neat way for preschoolers to share songs and stories with their families!

Here's a cute poem and song to use with the Story Glove. Have fun and let your imagination run wild!

Little Angel Watching Me

(Patterns you'll need: an angel and a heart)

> **Little angel watching me,** *(attach angel)*
>
> **You're as cute as you can be!** *(Wiggle your finger)*
>
> **God sent you from up above** *(wave your finger in the air)*
>
> **To care for me with your sweet love!** *(Attach heart)*

Mr. Noah Built an Ark

(Patterns you'll need: man, boat, sheep, cow, and dove) Sing the following song to the tune of "Old MacDonald" as you attach the pictures to your Story Glove.

> **Mr. Noah built and ark—** *(attach man and boat)*
>
> **Howdy-howdy-doo!**
>
> **And on the ark there was a cow—** *(attach cow)*
>
> **Howdy-howdy-doo!**
>
> **With a moo-moo here**
>
> **And a moo-moo there.**
>
> **Here a moo, there a moo**
>
> **Ev'rywhere a moo-moo!**
>
> **Mr. Noah built and ark-**
>
> **Howdy-howdy-doo!**

(Continue in the same way using the sheep and the dove.)

> Preschool kids love using Story Gloves to tell familiar stories including The Little Red Hen, Goldilocks and the Three Bears, and the Christmas story of Jesus' birth. Provide these together times often. Consider using old coloring books, magazines, children's story Bibles, and storybooks for colorful pictures in a snap!

SUPER SONGS

What's the flip-side of great stories? Super songs! And preschoolers love songs, rhythm 'n rhyme, and musical instruments. Every good preschool program contains song time—but a great preschool offers music! What's the difference? Songs are just sung words, but music expands into a much broader category, including: musical instruments, rhythm sticks, rhythm ribbons, and in general, more than just singing words. Music is as much a feeling as it is an auditory experience, and even preschoolers are as equally delighted by musical sounds as by specific lyrics.

When considering how to implement songs and music into your preschool program, be sure to think of the three R's: rhythm, rhyme, and repetition. Rhythm is the active portion of music, and perfectly suited for little wiggle-worms. Rhyme captures a preschooler's sense of fun and fascination with letter sounds. And repetition keeps music and song memorably alive. Provide songs and music that have simple words and tunes, then look for ways to activate preschool songs-that is, make them lively, action-filled, and engaging. Try adding motions to lyrics, letting children bang and bop on "musical instruments" around the class, leading the class in lively marches, or waving ribbons and batons in time to various tunes. Active songs stay active in the mind long after the last notes fade!

In this section, you'll discover a myriad of methods to incorporate into your songs and music. And there are specific songs listed and new songs to old tunes composed for your singing enjoyment. Have fun as you put joyous melodies in your preschooler's hearts.

CREATIVE MOVEMENT TO MUSIC

Can you think of a particular song that always seems to get your toes tapping and your head bopping? Now that's a super song! Songs and tunes that create motion fill us and invite us to become part of the music. It's not just our ears or voices that are engaged—our whole being seems to thump in time to the rhythm. Music is as natural to creative movement as lemons are to lemonade. And preschoolers are as natural to movement as they are to breathing. The perfect match! Nearly all songs and music lend themselves to movement of one sort or another. For instance, lively songs and music invite high-stepping marches, bouncing feet, and clapping hands. Slower songs make children swing and sway, and relax and rock.

Encouraging creative movement helps preschoolers develop motor skills, coordination, and self-confidence. And getting with partners makes "movin' and groovin' " to the music even more fun. So what kinds of creative movement are there? Plenty! Here is a list of creative movement ideas to offer your preschoolers.

❋ *Waving scarves or long crepe paper streamers in time to music.*

❋ *"Rowing" a pretend boat with a partner.*

❋ *Acting out animals or butterflies or birds in time to music, such as for Easter or springtime songs.*

❋ *Tiptoeing along masking tape lines to slow, restful music.*

❋ *Coloring in time to the rhythm of the music.*

❋ *"Finger-dancing" and clapping in rhythm.*

Creative movement is just that: *creative*. Let children move and express themselves freely and creatively. The sense of enjoyment and musical appreciation you're creating now will last children for a lifetime.

Making Musical Instruments

Taa-daa-daaaa! How many impromptu musical instruments can your preschoolers create? Rapping on floors, bopping on books, dinging on wastebaskets, and even clinking on file cabinets make beautiful sounds and give young children creative outlets. Musical instruments have been around since the dawn of mankind. Why? They're expressive. They're creative. They're versatile. And most of all…they're fun!

You and your preschoolers can make a variety of lively, musical instruments to play. Directions for several instruments are given below. Keep musical instruments in the ***Super Story & Song Box*** for "instant instrumental" accompaniments all year long. Then send the children's instruments home at the end of the year.

Tambourines— You'll need aluminum pie plates, construction paper, tape, uncooked beans, duct tape, and scissors. Hand each child two pie plates. Have them decorate the bottoms of the plates by taping on scraps of colorful construction paper. Then hand each child several uncooked beans. Place the beans between the insides of the pie plates, then tape around the edges of the plates using duct tape. Now you're set to shake, rattle, and roll!

Squeeky Kazoos— You'll need disposable plastic cups, crepe paper, scissors, tape, and plastic drinking straws. Before class, carefully put a small slit in the bottom of each disposable plastic cup. Hand each child a disposable plastic cup and a plastic drinking straw. Show children how to tape crepe paper streamers to one end of each drinking straw. Help children insert the plain ends the drinking straws through the slits in the bottoms of the cups. When the straws are moved up and down, there should be loud squeeks and squawks. Jab n' jam your Squeeky Kazoos up and down in time to music.

Tootle-Toots— You'll need cardboard tubes, waxed paper clear tape, markers, curling ribbon, and scissors. Be sure you have a cardboard tube for each child. Empty bathroom tissue tubes or halves of paper towel tubes work great. Precut five inch squares of waxed paper and six inch pieces of curling ribbon. Curl the ribbons with the edge of your scissors.

Hand each child a tube and a square of waxed paper. Invite children to decorate the tubes with markers. Then help children place the waxed paper squares over one end of each tube, and tape the squares in place. Then have children tape on pieces of curling ribbon to finish decorating their Tootle-Toot tubes.

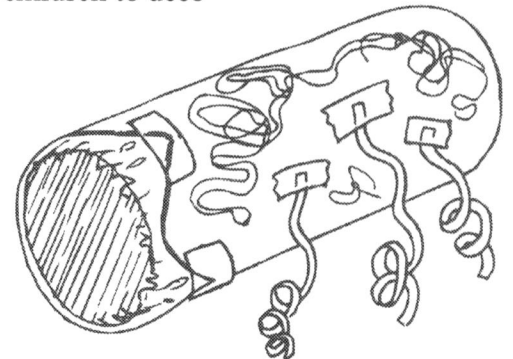

When the tubes are finished, let children practice humming through the open ends much like a kazoo. Then use your Tootle-Toots in a lively marching band or as back-up for any song.

Jingle Bell Bouncers— You'll need one inch wide ribbon, jingle bells, narrow ribbon in a variety of color, tape, and scissors. Please make sure the jingle bells are larger than a fifty-cent piece to avoid and choking hazards. You'll need one to three large jingle bells for each child.

Before class, cut an eighteen inch length of wide ribbon for each child. You'll also need to cut a pile of five inch long narrow ribbon in various colors.

Hand each child one, two, or three jingle bells and a length of wide ribbon. Help children tie the bells on the ribbon at equal intervals. If you have only one bell per child, tie it in the center of the ribbon. If you have a large group, recruit adult helpers or tie the bells to the ribbons before class.

When the bells are attached, invite children to tape a rainbow of ribbons to the end of each wide ribbon. Hold the other end of the ribbon and shake and bounce the jingle bells. What a pretty chorus of jingles and jangles!

ACTION SONGS

Songs with accompanying motions and actions are in perfect harmony with lively preschoolers. And even better news? Nearly all preschool songs can be turned into active, involving fun times. Look for actions that naturally go with lyrics. Arm circles, toe touches, tapping tummies, and acting out lyrics are easily introduced into most songs. For a fun twist, add props to enhance the actions. For example, swaying scarves, swooping paper streamers, and even crinkling and snapping paper work well as large motor motions. Teaching children how to use sign language in simple songs is another example of adding action to song lyrics. Read on to discover how to make up your own new songs complete with actions and motions!

OLD FAVORITES—NEW WORDS

Familiar tunes from childhood songs are as perennial as the grass—and a lot more colorful! How many old tunes can you hum? There's "The Farmer in the Dell," "Old MacDonald," "Mulberry Bush," "London Bridge," "Did You Ever See a Lassie," and bunches more. Great melodies that have lasted years and will be around for eons to come. Why? Because they're simple, sing-song tunes that contain repetitive melodies. These childhood songs are especially great for preschool teachers. Why? Because they fall into the song category known as "public domain." That is, anyone can use their tunes and rewrite the words and not infringe on any copyrights. In other words, you can rewrite the words to "Mary Had a Little Lamb" and not step on anyone's toes—or fear reprisal from copyright attorneys. This opens the door wide for custom-made songs and ditties for your little ones. And you can add as many or as few actions as you'd like! A sampling of familiar tunes with new words and actions are given below. Sing these through, then make up a songbook of your own!

Jesus Is Our Friend (tune: "London Bridge")

**Jesus is our friend today!
Clap your hands—shout, "Hooray!"** *(clap your hands)*
**Jesus is our friend today!
We love Jesus!**

**Jesus is our friend today!
Stomp your feet—shout, "Hooray!"** *(stomp your feet)*
**Jesus is our friend today!
We love Jesus!**

**Jesus is our friend today!
Turn around—shout, "Hooray!"** *(turn around in place)*
**Jesus is our friend today!
We love Jesus!**

(Add more actions such as tap your nose, tippytoe, and jump up high.)

Busy Bee (tune: "Row Your Boat")

Sweep, sweep, sweep the floor— *(pretend to sweep the floor)*
Be a busy bee!
Help awhile, you'll bring a smile *(point to your smile)*
To all your fam-i-ly!

Rake, rake, rake the yard— *(pretend to rake)*
Be a busy bee!
Help awhile, you'll bring a smile *(point to your smile)*
To all your fam-i-ly!

Wash, wash, wash, your hands— *(pretend to wash your hands)*
Be a busy bee!
Help awhile, you'll bring a smile *(point to your smile)*
To all your fam-i-ly!

The Prayer Song (tune: "Jesus Loves Me")

You can talk to God each day, *(point upward)*
When you bow your head and pray. *(fold your hands and bow your head)*
God will always answer you— *(nod your head)*
He loves your prayer and loves you, too. *(cover your heart with your hands)*

Please pray to God— *(fold your hands)*
Please pray to God— *(fold your hands)*
Please pray to God— *(fold your hands)*
And tell God, "I love you." *(cover your heart with your hands)*

Do You Know Who's On the Ark?

(tune: "Did You Ever See a Lassie?")

Do you know who's on the ark, the ark, the ark?
Do you know who's on the ark just a-sailing a-long?
With a hee-haw, hee-haw, hee-haw, hee-haw. *(make donkey ears with your hands)*
Do you know who's on the ark just sailing a-long?

Do you know who's on the ark, the ark, the ark?
Do you know who's on the ark just a-sailing a-long?
With a me-ow, me-ow, me-ow, me-ow. *(meow like a cat)*
Do you know who's on the ark just sailing a-long?

Do you know who's on the ark, the ark, the ark?
Do you know who's on the ark just a-sailing a-long?
With a cock-a-doodle-doo, a cock-a-doodle-doo. *(crow and flap like a rooster)*
Do you know who's on the ark just sailing a-long?

(Add other animals and birds along with appropriate actions.)

Let children make animal masks to wear as they sing and act out the various animals on the ark!

SONG POSTERS

We all know that young children crave colorful pictures with stories—and songs aren't any different. Colorful pictures and posters add so much to songs and help children remember the lyrics as well. But where do these pictures and posters come from? Good old-fashioned coloring books or old storybooks for a start. Simply color pictures from a coloring book, then glue or tape them to a large sheet of colorful poster board. Be sure the pictures are large enough for a group of preschoolers to see when they're sitting in a circle. As you sing, point to the appropriate pictures on your poster and give children a visual treat as they sing along. And if you cover your posters in clear, self-adhesive paper, they'll last for years.

Another way to illustrate songs is by using overhead transparencies. These can be prepared in two ways: either by drawing a picture directly on a transparency, or by photocopying a ready-made picture onto a transparency. Either way, transparencies can be colored using permanent markers. Then shine the transparency on a wall as you sing. Transparencies are inexpensive, last forever, and store easily in a file folder.

The Special Secrets Box

Is it really all right to keep secrets?

Yes, when it's for a special gift! And the items, ideas, and organizational tips in this box are like special gifts for any preschool teacher and class. Making class time run smoother and more efficiently while adding small elements of surprise make this diminutive box dynamite!

How can the element of surprise make a difference?

Since you're a preschool teacher, you already know your day is full of unexpected surprises. In fact, you've probably come to expect them! Bumped knees, uncovered sneezes, wet pants, flowers for the teacher, smiles, and hugs. Some delightful surprises and a few "oh-no's." But it's the element of surprise that keeps little ones anxiously awaiting the next exciting activity, the next delightful song, the next delicious snack. And you can encourage that sense of excitement with a special box full of tricks-of-the-trade, rainy day surprises, great goodies, and super organizational ideas. All of these are key in creating a sense of "sanity" while teaching preschoolers.

Before we move into the Secret Box and discover the fun waiting inside, let's look at 6 Key Qualities you'll need in keeping your sanity while teaching preschool!

Sense of humor

Awesome organization

Nurturing attitude

Inventive spirit

Tireless energy

Yielding and flexible disposition

Each of these important qualities is guaranteed help make (and keep) you a memorable, loving teacher—even during those unexpected surprises! Each letter in the acronym for "SANITY" will be discussed in the following pages along with items from the Secret Box that help in each category. Have fun collecting items for your Secret Box and remember: the secret is in the "SANITY!"

What's in the box?

The chart on page 103 lists the fun you'll find in each category of the Special Secrets Box. You'll find the directions for making or preparing the items in the chart within this chapter. Have fun collecting the special items for this all-important box in the Sanity Savers system!

S	A	N	I	T	Y
* Rainy Day Bag	* Fabulous Folders	* Thumbody Special Necklace	* Mr. Hugga Bear	* Line-Em-Up Rope	* Transition Tricks
* Modeling Dough Mania	* General Info Folder	* Rainbow Ribbons	* Terrific Tickets	* Hand Holders	* Pompom Pointer
* Chenille Wire Creations	* Substitute Folder	* Special Stickers	* Shapes 'n Circles	* Noisemakers	* Music Box
* Funny Flannel Board Songs	* Cubbies 'n Cubes	* Birthday Box		* Time Out Banner	
				* Simple Snacks	

Sense of Humor

Oh, my! Here comes Jennie—the preschool cyclone. Perpetual motion captured in one tiny dynamo. You wonder, "How can such a little girl have so much energy?" She runs across the room to give you a hug, but…*crash!* Down goes your favorite vase and all the flowers Timmy just brought you. What happens next? You:

A. go to pieces like the vase.

B. hand sobbing Jennie a broom and a bundle of guilt.

C. laugh.

And the answer is…C! Wait a minute-you laugh? But Jennie's crying and Timmy's looking at Jennie as if she may be a beetle! *How can I laugh,* you ask? Because there's nothing that will mend your vase—yet there are words that could break a child's heart over this insignificant incident. Nothing heals hurt like humor. Nothing lifts hearts like laughter. Your smiles and sense of humor assure young children that they're "okay" and greatly loved. Preschoolers find security in smiles and love in laughter, so be generous with both! Jesus gave us such a gift when he told us to bring our burdens to him and he'd lighten our loads. Preschoolers have heavy loads, too, and your sense of humor lightens those loads and offers acceptance. Besides, a healthy sense of humor will maintain your positive outlook and nurture your patience.

Rainy Day Bag

What situations call for a great sense of humor? Rainy days, extra-long preschool sessions, sickness, accidents—in general, any and all situations! The items and ideas in this portion of the *Super Secrets Box* will help you and your children keep smiles on your faces and laughter in your hearts.

Rainy days can be especially trying. Dank dreariness can mean whiny weariness. Any seasoned teacher knows well the Law of Kid-Weather: when barometric pressure falls, kids' kinesthetic pressure rises! To keep your sense of humor during those indoor playtimes, you need the secret weapons included in the Rainy Day Bag. Collect the following items to use on rainy or snowy days.

- plastic or metal mini-cars, trucks, boats, and airplanes
- animal and people figurines
- plastic, pull-apart eggs with mini-suprises inside
- rubber stampers and a water-based ink pad
- neon markers or crayons

Keeping a sense of humor helps children see the positive sides of even mistakes or accidents.

- small dolls with hair to comb
- a magnifying glass
- a stethoscope

Be on the lookout for other small, unique items to place in the Rainy Day Bag. Check garage sales, thrift stores, and toy close-out shops. The excitement isn't in the toys themselves, but in letting your surprises out of the bag *only* during inclement weather!

Also included in the sense of humor portion of the *Super Secrets Box* is modeling dough. Be sure to include vinyl placemats and a variety of clever cookie cutters, plastic knives, and empty spools. Place the cutters in a plastic margarine container and allow only as many children to play with the dough as there are placemats. Take turns often so no one feels left out. Prepare your own modeling dough with the recipe included here or purchase ready-made dough. Keeping handy the ingredients for making edible modeling dough is a real treat on rainy days! The recipe for this delicious dough is also included here.

Marvellous Modeling Dough

Heat almost to boiling 1 1/2 cups water and 1/2 cup salt. Remove from heat and add 2 Tbls. vegetable oil, 2 Tbls. alum, and food coloring if desired. Cool until mixture is easy to handle. Knead in 2-3 cups of flour. Continue to knead until soft and pliable. Store in a resealable bag or plastic container for up to two weeks.

Incredible-Edible Modeling Dough

In a large bowl, mix 3 cups of smooth peanut butter and 2 cups of powdered sugar. Mix until the mixture forms a doughy ball. Knead the dough until it's smooth. It the sough is sticky, add more powdered sugar. If the dough is crumbly, add a bit of milk. Store the dough in a sealed plastic bag. Edible dough stays yummy for several days.

> Invite preschoolers to help make modeling clay—they love kneading the tactile dough!

Chennile Wire Creations

Chenille wires make for great fun on rainy days. Encourage children to create goofy glasses to wear, bend the wires into animal shapes, or wind them around colored tissue paper for fanciful flowers to brighten the day.

Funny Flannel Board Songs

Last but not least, include a selection of silly songs and flannel board pictures to tickle dreary-day funny bones. The old camp favorite, "Agalina, Hagalina" is a sure winner. This totally silly song is preschool-perfect and smiles and giggles are guaranteed to erupt. Sing or chant the song words as you "build" a funny face using yarn and construction paper. Words and directions are included here. Then there's "5 Little Ducks," a delightful rhyme that gets kids counting and quacking! And another great flannel board treat is "The Old Lady Who Swallowed a Fly." Kids cackle with delight over this buggy-tale of an old lady who gobbled a bug—and plenty of other odd items. Again, words and a duck pattern are provided. Be on the search for other cute, crazy, or classic songs, rhymes, and poems to illustrate and present on a flannel board.

> **Helpful Hints**
>
> Plastic drinking straws, cotton balls, and paper cups all make unusual "building materials." When any of these are used along with chenille wires, preschool imaginations soar!

Agalina Hagalina

Preparation: You'll need a colored yarn, scissors, colored construction paper. Cut a 12-inch pieces of yarn, a 5-inch piece of green yarn, a 5-inch piece of red yarn, and another 5-inch piece of yarn in any color. You'll also need to cut two 1 X 2-inch paper "teeth," a pair of goofy paper eyes, and a small paper "wart." Color one eye blue and the other eye green. Keep the pieces for this song in a letter envelope with a copy of the words.

Presentation: Sing or say the words as you "build" this funny face by following the directions in parentheses.

Chorus:
Agalina Hagalina *(make a "head" with the long piece of yarn)*
Oh-ka-to-ka, poke-a-woke-a,
Awk-a-talk-a-walk-a was her name.

There were two hairs on her head, *(place red and green yarn "hairs" on top of the head)*
One was green and the other was red.
(repeat chorus)

She had two eyes, green and blue— *(place paper eyes on the face)*
One looked at me and the other loked at you.
(repeat chorus)

There were two teeth in her mouth— *(place teeth on the face)*
One pointed north and the other pointed south.
(repeat chorus)

On her face there was a nose— *(make a funny nose)*
'Bout as long as a garden hose.
(repeat chorus)

On her nose there was a wart— *(place the wart on the nose)*
Of a ve-ry peculiar sort!
(repeat chorus)

Now you might think she's a silly head,
But you should see her cousin Fred!
(repeat chorus one last time)

5 Little Ducks

Preparation: You'll need the five copies of the duck pattern from page 108. Photocopy the ducks on white or yellow paper and glue a bit of felt on the back of each.

Presentation: Begin with all five ducks on the flannel board. The remove one duck at a time as you sing or say the words to the rhyme. Follow the directions in parentheses.

5 little ducks went out to play— *(hold up 5 fingers)*

"Quack, quack, quack," they sang all day! *(Cup hands and clap 3 times)*

One little duck splish-splashed away— *(brush hands together 2 times)*

Then there were 4 little ducks. *(Hold up 4 fingers)*

(Repeat using 4, 3, 2, then 1 little duck)

Permission to photocopy for church, school, or home use only.
Taken from *Sanity Savers*
© Susan Lingo, Susan Lingo Books, 2007.

The Old Lady Who Swallowed a Fly

Preparation: You'll need coloring book pictures of a farmer's wife, a horse, a cow, a dog, a cat, and a bird. You'll also need tangled thread to represent the "fly." Color the pictures and attach a bit of felt to the back of each so they'll stick to the flannel board.

Presentation: Read the following story and place pictures of the underlined words on the flannel board. Point to each picture as you repeat the story. Encourage children to repeat the words with you.

There was an old <u>lady</u> who swallowed a <u>fly</u>.
I don't know why she swallowed a fly.
Poor old lady—please eat a pie!

There was an old lady who swallowed a <u>bird</u>.
How absurd, she swallowed a bird!
She swallowed the bird to catch the fly.
I don't know why she swallowed a fly.
Poor old lady—please eat a pie!

There was an old lady who swallowed a <u>cat</u>.
Imagine that, she swallowed a cat!
She swallowed the cat to catch the bird, she swallowed the bird to catch the fly.
I don't know why she swallowed a fly.
Poor old lady—please eat a pie!

Preschoolers love stories, rhymes, and songs that repeat words and lists—plus, it helps them learn the skill of sequencing!

There was an old lady who swallowed a <u>dog</u>.
She went the whole hog when she swallowed a dog!
She swallowed the dog to catch the cat, she swallowed the cat to catch the bird, she swallowed the bird to catch the fly.
I don't know why she swallowed a fly.
Poor old lady—please eat a pie!

There was an old lady who swallowed a <u>cow</u>.
I don't know how she swallowed a cow!
She swallowed the cow to catch the dog, she swallowed the dog to catch the cat, she swallowed the cat to catch the bird, she swallowed the bird to catch the fly.
I don't know why she swallowed a fly.
Poor old lady—please eat a pie!

There was an old lady who swallowed a <u>horse</u>.
She was full of course when she swallowed that horse!
She swallowed the horse to catch the cow, she swallowed the cow to catch the dog, she swallowed the dog to catch the cat, she swallowed the cat to catch the bird, she swallowed the bird to catch the fly.
I don't know why she swallowed a fly.
Poor old lady—*please eat a pie!*

Awesome Organization

A place for everything and everything in it's place. An effective axiom for organization in and out of the classroom. Without a good system for organization you'd hopelessly fumble for papers, lists, equipment, and supplies. You'd puzzle over what to do next without organized lesson plans. And you'd worry about what a substitute might or might not do in your absence. Organization. You simply can't be without it. And just as any profession has tricks of the trade, so do teaching and classroom organization.

Fabulous Folders

The first step in awesome organization are the key folders you prepare and keep as part of your *Super Secret Box*: the **General Information folder** and the **Substitute folder**. Both keep anyone in charge of your class actively in charge of any situation. The General Information folder is designed for the regular classroom teacher. It contains a class list, a lesson-plan page, a welcome letter to the parents, and a letter of welcome to preschoolers. You'll find these reproducible helps on pages 111 to 114. Photocopy them, fill in essential information, and place them in a colorful pocket folder labeled "General Information." Keep the folder in your *Super Secret Box* for quick referral, and be sure to add new or additional information throughout the year.

Your **Substitute folder** is an invaluable aid for anyone needing to cover for you in your absence. The folder contains the class list, helpful people in the church to call for questions or to help in an emergency, a copy of the class schedule and a list of activities to do, the exit route in case of fire, and the location of your storm shelter or safe site in case of bad weather. You'll also want to include a blank page for notes the substitute might write for you. The reproducible forms are found on pages 115 through 117. Photocopy them, fill in the information, and place them in a colorful pocket folder labeled "Substitute Folder." You may want to tuck a colorful storybook in the folder for quick reading to the class. Keep the folder in your *Super Secret Box* and inform your substitute of where to find this important information.

Preschool Class List for _____ (year)

Teacher: _____

Assistants: _____

Child's Name	Parent's Name	Phone Number

Permission to photocopy for church, school, or home use only. Taken from *Sanity Savers*
© Susan Lingo, Susan Lingo Books, 2007.

LESSON PLANS

	Sunday	Monday	Tuesday	Wednesday	Thursday	Friday
Arrival						
Bible Lesson						
Bible Story						
Craft						
Game						
Songs						
Snack						
Supplies						

Permission to photocopy for church, school, or home use only. Taken from *Sanity Savers*
© Susan Lingo, Susan Lingo Books, 2007.

Dear Parent,

I'd like to welcome you and your child to my class. We'll be having lots of fun this year learning about God, about ourselves, and about the people and world around us. Please feel free to stop by for a visit any time—and your help during the year will be greatly appreciated. My phone number is _____.
Feel free to call whenever you have questions or concerns.

Sincerely,

_____

Dear _____,

My name is _____. and I will be your teacher this year. I'm so glad we'll be together. I know you'll have lots of fun and meet many new friends. I look forward to seeing you soon!

Love,

_____

Permission to photocopy for church, school, or home use only. Taken from *Sanity Savers*
© Susan Lingo, Susan Lingo Books, 2007.

Here is the route you'll need to take in case of a fire or fire drill. Follow the arrows.

If you need assistance, ask: _____

Here is the route to the safest place to be in case of a bad storm. Follow the arrows.

If you need assistance, ask: _____

SUBSTITUTE INFORMATION

Hi, and welcome to our class! Here's a collection of helpful information including the class schedule, roster, and possible activities. If you need help or assistance, please ask: _____.

SCHEDULE

From _____ to _____ we have _____
From _____ to _____ we have _____
From _____ to _____ we have _____
From _____ to _____ we have _____
From _____ to _____ we have _____
From _____ to _____ we have _____
From _____ to _____ we have _____

CLASS ROSTER

- _____
- _____
- _____
- _____
- _____
- _____

- _____
- _____
- _____
- _____
- _____
- _____

POSSIBLE ACTIVITIES

Bible story/lesson: _____
Craft: _____
Game: _____
Snack: _____
Songs: _____

Please refer to the Creative Crafts Box, the Great Games Box, and the Super Story & Song Box for more ideas and supplies!

Permission to photocopy for church, school, or home use only. Taken from *Sanity Savers*
© Susan Lingo, Susan Lingo Books, 2007.

Cubbies and Cubes

In addition to the General Information and Substitute Folders, cubbies and storage cubicles are invaluable musts for organization. Cubicles for children allow you to send home artwork and important papers, gives parents a place to check for notes and such, and offers children a "place of their own." Cubbies and storage cubicles can be simply made in a variety of ways. One of the easiest, is to cut the ends from half-gallon milk cartons and duct tape the cartons together to make rows of "cubby holes." Cover the outside edges of the cubbies with colorful self-adhesive paper. Then tape a name card for each child to the bottom of each cubby.

Another way to assemble individual storage areas is to purchase a ready-made shoe

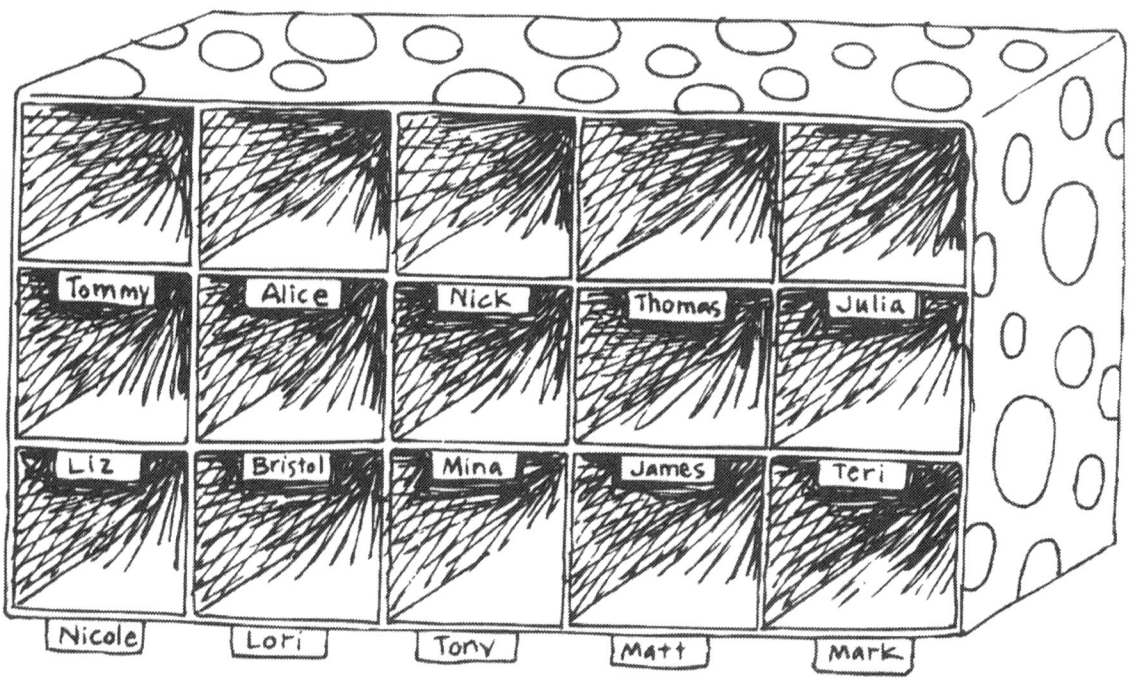

storage box. These special boxes are available at most discount stores and are in the department that sells under-the-bed storage boxes. Assemble the box, add name cards, and...viola! Instant cubbies. Plastic tubs make sturdy, portable cubbies and even paper shopping bags with handles will work—and kids have fun decorating and personalizing them. The important things isn't what individual cubbies and storage cubicles are made from, it's the fact that you've provided a personal place for preschooler's belongings, and shows you value them as individuals. And this brings us to the third letter in the acronym for SANITY: the letter N which stands for "Nurturing."

Nurturing Spirit

According to Erik H. Erikson's developmental theory for childhood emotions, the two big emotional turning points in a child's early life are: autonomy (self-sufficiency and trust), and initiative (confidence and a sense of "go-getter"). As preschoolers experience the power of doing and deciding, their sense of autonomy blossoms. And as they feel more independent and capable, initiative moves into full swing. Autonomy and initiative are key factors in a preschooler's security and sense of self, and it's vital to nurture these budding rudiments of self-esteem. Through sincere affirmations, a listening ear (and heart), and an attitude of "you're special to God and precious to me," you draw near your children and help them feel a sense of deep worth. The ideas and items included in this portion of the Secret Box are designed to help you tell your preschoolers they're precious and special.

Thumbody Special Necklace

One of the simplest, most effective affirmations I stumbled on while teaching preschool, was the "Thumbody Special" necklace of honor. I found a wonderful, giant rubber thumb in the candy section of the grocery store. It was a novel wrapping for a candy sucker, but the thumb itself held the sweetest treasure! I threaded fishing line through the end of the rubber and turned it into the "Thumbody Special" necklace. Each time my preschoolers arrived, I'd watch for someone doing or saying something especially encouraging to a friend. For example, it might be handing a friend a block they needed to finish a tower. Or sharing crayons without being told. Or patting a friend who had fallen. I'd quietly place the "Thumbody Special" necklace on that child to proudly wear. Then lo and behold, guess what happened? One day, a child wearing the necklace noticed someone being kind and handed the necklace to that child to wear! Wow! Not only did the simple necklace nurture self-esteem and kindness, it helped children notice and thank others for being kind as well.

The "Thumbody Special" necklace is an example of how simple, inexpensive items can be used to nurture affirmations in the classroom. Check the candy counter for a super selection of other novelties that, with a little imagination, can be turned into cute wearable affirmations. One note: do keep track of who has worn the affirmation and be sure each child is affirmed more than once. Encourage children to "award" the honor to others whenever they notice an act of kindness or kind words being spoken.

Rainbow Ribbons

Also included in the nurturing section of the Secret Box is a roll of blue or rainbow colored ribbon and a scissors. Clip off six-inch sections of ribbon to hand children as special "anytime gifts." Attach pretty stickers to one end of each ribbon for an extra neat touch. Encourage children to collect their ribbons and keep them in their Bibles as bookmarks.

Special Stickers

Stickers also make wonderful, inexpensive ways to say "you're special" to preschoolers. But be careful about attaching stickers to clothing. Sometimes they're overlooked and go through the was which ruins the stickers and possibly the fabric! Place stickers on the backs of preschoolers' hands or on small pieces of paper to take home.

Birthday Box

One final important item in the Secret Box is called the Birthday Box. This wonderful box holds a treasure trove of preschool delights for the "birthday child." Whenever you celebrate a child's birthday, let him or her choose a fun "gift" from the Birthday Box. Gifts might include combs and brushes, barrettes, mini cars and trucks, tiny packs of crayons, pencils, small books, fast-food coupons, small boxes of raisins, and assorted toys and games. Check party stores for a non-stop collection of items to include. And if you have children whose birthdays are in the summer or at times when you don't regularly meet, be sure to allow them to choose an item in the month closest their special day!

INVENTIVE IDEAS

Look in the Thesaurus under the heading "inventive." What words are listed? "Clever," "resourceful," "bright," "able," "creative," and "preschool teacher." Well, maybe preschool teacher isn't a technical listing-but it is a practical synonym for the word "inventive." When needs must, ideas drive. What a perfect axiom to describe the inventive spirit a preschool teacher needs on a daily basis! Constantly on the lookout for fresh, exciting ways to teach. Always searching for better organizational tips. Eagerly seeking unique methods of involving young charges. And the items in this portion of the *Super Secrets Box* will help you be more inventive—especially Mr. Hugga Bear.

Mr. Hugga Bear

Mr. Hugga Bear is a fuzzy, cuddly teddy kept in the Secret Box for times when kids need a little extra TLC, companionship, and security. Teary-eyed times, small hurts and mishaps, when Mommy's a little late, or other times young children need a friend to hold, Mr. Hugga Bear is ready and willing. To make Mr. Hugga Bear, simply purchase a ready-made teddy from a toy or craft store. Tie a bright, puffy bow around the teddy's neck and glue a red felt heart on the teddy's tummy. Now Mr. Hugga Bear is ready to give warm comfort to your preschoolers.

Terrific Tickets

Tickets are a great novelty to add to your Secret Box—and kids of all ages love 'em. Large rolls of tickets can be purchased at party and office stores, and many discount centers. Or make your own tickets using the pattern provided here. Simply photocopy the pattern on stiff colored paper and cut them out. Keep your tickets in a large envelope inside the Secret Box. Use tickets as a fun twist for visiting activity centers, as a way to invite children to story time, or as a great way to get preschoolers in a line for the drinking fountain.

Shapes 'n Circles

Invent a bunch o' games with colored shapes and circles that you store in the Secret Box. Cover colored poster board or construction paper with clear, self-adhesive paper. Then cut out a variety of shapes in several sizes. Be sure there are sets of matching shapes included. Cut out three large circles in yellow, red, and green to use as a "traffic lights."

Now, with all your shapes, colors, and traffic lights, don your inventor's cap and brainstorm as many games and activities as you can on a slip of paper! How many did you invent? Here are several ideas that might get you thinking. Use the stop lights to play "Red Light, Green Light." Use three traffic sign to help control indoor noise levels. The green light represents a good noise level—let's keep going as is. Yellow stands for "Caution-it's getting a little loud. Let's go back to green." And red is "Stop! It's too noisy. We need to go back to green." For the various shapes, hide them around the room and go on a safari hunt. Use the shapes to help children find partners for a game or special activity. Tape the shapes to the floor and play Tip Toe to the Triangles." Play a musical chairs-type game using shapes and colors. Let children choose shapes and colors from a paper bag. Then play "What Am I?" by giving clues to help others guess. See? You can invent a gaggle of games and activities in a flash with these simple paper props!

Tireless Energy

Few people have as much boundless energy as teachers of young children. And as fast as preschoolers move, their teachers must always be one step ahead! It's this tireless energy that makes for great teachers, so they say. But let's get real! Even the most hyperactive, energetic preschool teachers become tired—or weary. The items included in this section of the Secret Box will help give you tips on making those little tiring efforts, much less taxing.

Lining preschoolers up doesn't sound like such a big deal. After all, these are little kids, right? Well butterflies are little too, but have ever tried to get twenty of them to stop fluttering simultaneously? Not so simple! And it's "little" tasks like these that are the most tiring for any teacher. But two incredibly simple items in the Secret Box can be your secret to saving precious energy! The Line 'Em Up rope and the Hand-Holder are designed to be easy, effective aids to lining up preschoolers and keeping them safe and comfortable.

Line 'Em Up Rope

The Line 'Em Up rope can be made from any jump rope or thick jute rope. Tie knots at twelve inch intervals down the entire length. You may need several ropes if your group is large. Either tie the ropes together or make two smaller ones. When you want children to line up, help them each find a knot to hold. The children will be evenly spaced to prevent accidental pushing or bumping, and you can easily count your kids when they're in line.

Hand-Holders

The Hand-Holder is a clever devise made from the plastic rings that hold six packs of soda pop. Cut the rings so they're in sets of two connected rings. Tape a short streamer of blue, red, yellow, or green ribbon to the piece connecting the rings. This color-coding system will be explained in a moment. When you want children to find walking partners or line up in pairs, have each child hold onto a plastic ring. Group the children according to their colors. This is a great way to keep kids organized, to make smaller groups for walks, games, and other small group activities.

Noisemakers

Another energy saver is the use of audio signals for catching preschoolers' attention. Bells, whistles, clickers and clackers, and any other noise making devises can be used as "quiet signals" that will save your voice and capture attention. Tell children that when they hear the quiet signal, they're to look at you. Vary the noise making signals often to keep attention fresh, focused, and fun.

Time-Out Banner

Need a quick pick-me-up for you and your kids? Whip out the "Time Out Banner" and wave it around the room. March around the room with your banner held high and encourage children to join your special "parade." When everyone is in line, march once around the room, then settle down in one area. Read a colorful story, present a new song, share about what makes each child happy, or munch a special treat. The change of pace will zip up your energy and calm down your preschoolers. Make the Time Out Banner from a rectangle of colored fabric or bright construction paper. Write the words "Time Out!" on the banner and decorate the banner with smiley faces.

Simple Snacks

Last but not least, include a box of animal crackers or teddy shaped graham crackers in the Secret Box. This inexpensive treat is a sure pick-me-up when you need a little energy boost. The fun part: the cookies are for you—the kids just think you're doing something special for them!

> Steer clear of sugary snacks as they may make some children very active. Opt for small crackers, raisins, or pretzels to keep in your *Super Secrets Box*.

Yielding and Flexible Disposition

A yielding disposition is one in which you remain flexible and comfortable with last minute changes. It's the ability to turn on a dime—without losing your "cents." To be yielding you have to toss out rigidity, stubbornness, and a lot of ego. You need to think quick, make decisions in a flash, and think of the other person. A yielding and flexible preschool teacher goes with the flow instead of fighting like an upstream salmon. So what if story time is a little late? Does it really matter if the children don't quite remember every word to the song you're singing? Is it such a big thing that the crafts didn't turn out like the picture in the craft book? No! Being yielding and flexible means these and countless other unplanned events don't throw off your entire day. There are a few simple-to-collect items in the Secret Box that can help with changes-both expected and unexpected. And all are designed to keep you flexible and yielding—and having fun with your children.

Transition Tricks

Transitions between activities are a real challenge for preschool teachers and require immense flexibility. Just because you want it to be story time doesn't always mean your kids are ready to put away their toys. Smooth transitions are like changing gears in an old truck. If you change gears too fast, the engine may stall and you'll go nowhere. If you shift too slowly, you'll be stuck in neutral. Finesse is the key. How do you shift gears in a smooth, easy manner to keep things rolling? Try some of the following ideas!

* **Give the "2-minute" signal.** Inform children that they have two minutes more to play (or paint or whatever the activity). Then tell them you'll flash the lights a few times and that's their signal to clean up. Be sure to help in the clean up.

* **Play a musical tape when it's time to switch activities.** Challenge your children to see if they can have everything picked up and sit in the circle (or at the table) by the time the song ends.

* **Role play to smooth transitions.** If children are playing, invite them to pretend they're toy shop keepers and need to clean their store. If children are going from snack time to story time, have them be basketball players and toss napkins in the wastebasket on the way to the story rug. If children have just finished making crafty butterflies and are ready for snacks, have them pretend to "fly" to the snack table.

* **Place colored shapes on children's chairs or on the story rug,** or wherever the next activity takes place. Tell children to think of their favorite color, then when you call that color, those children can find a shape to match and sit down.

Giving preschool children helper roles in the classroom can be a big step in your own flexible attitude. Many teachers seem to adopt an "only the teacher can do it" attitude. By letting children take active roles in helping, you lessen the burden on yourself and help them feel a sense of responsibility and self-worth. Watering plants, wiping tables, straightening chairs, and putting "snibbles" from the floor in the wastebasket are all good ways to let preschoolers help.

Pompom Pointer

Make a Pompon Pointer and let children tap each other to go to the restroom, get a drink, go to the story circle, or get up from naps. Purchase a ready-made pompon or make one by wrapping yarn around a four inch cardboard rectangle. Tie the middle of the yarn with a small piece of yarn, then clip the looped ends. Tie the pompon to a drinking straw or small dowel.

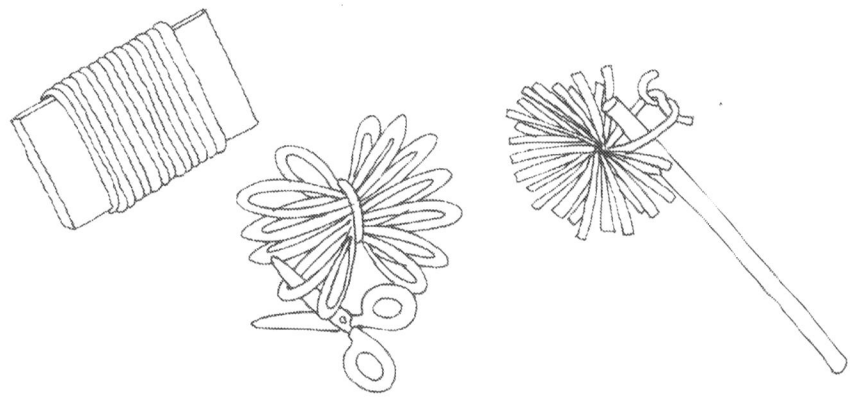

Music Box

Finally, a wind-up music box does wonders for transitional times and keeping kids flexible—and you relaxed. Wind up a music box and ask children to quietly go to the craft table, story rug, or wherever the next activity is to be held. Use the music box as a "cool down" time after outdoor playtimes, and as clean-up music after indoor play.

There you have it. The *Super Secrets Box*. But more important, you now have the whole arsenal of preschool teaching aids in a four-stage system which includes the ***Creative Crafts Box,*** the ***Great Games Box,*** the ***Super Story & Song Box,*** as well as the ***Super Secrets Box.*** Keep the boxes handy, add to them as your time and creativity permit, and have fun teaching the little ones God has placed in your tender care!

Looking for more great resources? You've come to the right place!

Object Talks

PRODUCT #	PRODUCT TITLE	PRICE PER ITEM	QUANTITY	TOTAL
1154-2	101 Simple Service Projects	$13.99		
1370-7	Quick Quiz Talk Starters	$13.99		
2022-4	Show Me! Devotions	$12.99		
7440-7	Show Me More! Object Talks	$12.99		
7441-7	20/20 Crafts & Object Talks	$10.99		
1417-7	Collect-n-Do Object Talks	$13.99		
1237-9	A to Z Object Talks (New Testament)	$5.99		
1236-0	A to Z Object Talks (Old Testament)	$5.99		
1838-X	Bible Message Make-n-Takes	$12.99		
1429-0	Preschool Bible Message Make-n-Takes	$12.99		
1184-4	Edible Object Talks (Jesus)	$5.99		
1183-6	Edible Object Talks (Values)	$5.99		

Crafts & Games

PRODUCT #	PRODUCT TITLE	PRICE PER ITEM	QUANTITY	TOTAL
7449-7	Larger-Than-Life Crafts & Service Projects	$10.99		
7441-7	20/20 Crafts & Object Talks	$10.99		
5695-7	Instant Games for Children's Ministry	$13.99		
1199-2	Collect-n-Play Games	$13.99		
1198-4	Collect-n-Make Crafts	$13.99		
1838-X	Bible Message Make-n-Takes	$12.99		

Bibles & Bible Storytelling

PRODUCT #	PRODUCT TITLE	PRICE PER ITEM	QUANTITY	TOTAL
7450-7	Kids-Tell-Em Bible Stories	$11.99		
0406-6	My Good Night Bible	$14.99		
1228-X	My Little Good Night Bible	$9.99		
1174-7	My Good Night StoryBook	$14.99		
1229-8	My Little Good Night StoryBook	$9.99		
1365-0	My Good Night Prayers	$14.99		
1522-X	Christmas With Night Light	$10.99		
1362-0	Bedtime for Night Light (coloring book)	$3.99		
1418-5	Collect-n-Tell Bible Stories	$13.99		

POWER BUILDERS (2-Year Curriculum)

PRODUCT #	PRODUCT TITLE	PRICE PER ITEM	QUANTITY	TOTAL
7550-7	Disciple Makers	$12.99		
7554-7	Faith Finders	$12.99		
7552-7	Servant Leaders	$12.99		
7556-7	Value Seekers	$12.99		
7551-7	Hope Finders	$12.99		
7555-7	Joy Builders	$12.99		
7557-7	Power Boosters	$12.99		
7553-7	Peace Makers	$12.99		

Teacher Ideas & Learning Centers

PRODUCT #	PRODUCT TITLE	PRICE PER ITEM	QUANTITY	TOTAL
5525-X	Saving Your Sanity (preschool)	$12.99		
7444-7	Instant Learning Fun-Folders OT (CD)	$9.99		
7445-7	Instant Learning Fun-Folders NT (CD)	$9.99		
1332-4	200+ Activities for Children's Ministry	$12.99		
7442-7	On & Off the Wall (Visual Teaching Tools)	$13.99		
7443-7	Classroom Celebrations!	$12.99		

Bible Memory, Bible Skills, & Worship Activities

PRODUCT #	PRODUCT TITLE	PRICE PER ITEM	QUANTITY	TOTAL
7446-7	Scripture Memory Makers	$12.99		
7445-7	Making Scripture Memorable	$12.99		
7448-7	Bible Skill Builders	$13.99		
7447-7	Worship Wow!	$12.99		

You can order two easy ways:

1. Directly from *Susan Lingo Books* through check or money order, or

2. from Amazon.com.

Send your check or money order (including shipping and handling) along with your order to:

Susan Lingo Books
3310 N. Logan Ave.
Loveland, CO 80538

Handling ($1.50 per order)	$1.50
Shipping: **Standard Book Rate:** 1-3 books—$10.50 4+ books—$12.00 + $1.50 each additional book **Priority USPS:** 1 book—$16.00 2+ books—$18.00 + $2.00 each additional book	
Subtotal of S/H	
Subtotal of books ordered	
TOTAL	

www.susanlingobooks.com

www.ingramcontent.com/pod-product-compliance
Lightning Source LLC
LaVergne TN
LVHW061312060426
835507LV00019B/2115